THAI COOKING COMPANION

SPICE OF LIFE

Text by Ekarin Yusuksomboon
Recipes by Intukarn Gajaseni Sirisant
Edited by Chris Baker

THAI COOKING COMPANION

Thai cooking means exciting tastes, alluring aromas, and beautifully designed dishes. But the heart of Thai cooking is something more: the freedom to create. This grows from the Thai spirit and Thai way of life. "Thai" means free. And Thais love their freedom. The Thai cook has the liberty to choose just the right ingredients to create the blend of sour, hot, salty and sweet tastes needed for perfection. Thai cuisine has absorbed influences from India, China, Arabia and Europe. But it has adapted these into its own totally distinctive style.

Each region of the kingdom has its own way of life which is reflected in its variant of the cuisine. But all share the same staple, rice, and all contribute to one country, one culture and one cuisine. In the kitchen and in the culture there is both harmony and contrast. Perhaps that is why Thais are so familiar with the spice of life.

The Thai people have worked the land for centuries and have built a special relationship with mother nature. Farming, and especially rice farming, is an integral part of the Thai way of life. The best-known Thai saying is "There are fish in the rivers and rice in the fields."

Life along the river

Start from the North of Thailand and the high hills bordering Burma. Travel down to the northeastern region of Esarn, where the majestic Mekong river divides Thailand from Laos. Drift through the brilliantly green paddy-fields of the Central Plains, the country's rice-bowl, down to the capital of Bangkok, one of the great cities of Asia. Set out for the brilliant beaches and sparkling waters of the Gulf of Thailand, and finally the South, where Thai culture mingles with Malay. In each region, the people and the natural environment have given birth to a special culture and a distinctive cuisine with its own local styles of cooking, flavors, and tastes.

The North : Warmth in the Mist

A sea of white mist hovers over the hills. Up here, in the fresh air among the tall forest trees, live many people who still prefer the coolness and solitude. Down below on the valley floor, the temperature is sub-tropical. There are towns and rice-fields. This is the Lanna kingdom of the north of Thailand—a blend of hill and valley, and of peoples from very different cultural background living together.

And eating together. Lanna people traditionally share food round a kuntoke. This is a small table made of oak—more like a tray with legs. Everyone likes to gather together in the evening, sitting on straw mats around the kuntoke, sharing their happiness and sorrows together, and sharing the very special dishes of Lanna.

Look on almost any kuntoke and you will find a chilli paste dip (nam phrik). It is the most basic Thai dish in all regions, and very adaptable. Most dips have a base of chilli and garlic, and then some salty or sweet tastes. They are eaten with fresh, par-boiled and deep-fried vegetables and fish. And often crispy pork skin (kaeb moo) as well.

In the north, the most famous chilli dips are nam phrik noom and nam phrik ong. Nam phrik noom is made with the large, yellow noom chilli. Nam phrik ong contains tomatoes. In other regions, the dips are made with shrimp paste, but in the north they use fermented whole soybeans instead, and this gives northern dips their distinctive flavour.

But there's more than chilli paste on the kuntoke—especially the creamy hung lay curries. Northern people love Burmese-style curry pastes with some pork fat, as in the soupy gaeng aom (curry of pork and innards). Northerners call all kinds of meat 'jin', so a famous chicken dish is yam jin gai (spicy northern-style chicken salad). The local curry, gaeng hoh (dried northern-style mixed curry), has an interesting origin. At festivals and charitable ceremonies, people give food to the monks. Afterwards, the leftovers are not thrown away but are fried together with curry paste, chopped lemongrass, chopped kaffir lime leaves, long beans, eggplants and vermicelli.

Delicious, but a bit oily. In the cooler temperature, the body needs some fat which is why northern food uses more coconut milk and animal fat. It provides energy and also keeps the skin moist. But if you are worried about cholesterol and weight, just use an old northern trick: eat some kratiem tone (single-cloved garlic) alongside oily dishes, because it has been proven to help reduce cholesterol in the blood vessels.

In the valleys of the north, the farmers grow both sticky and non-sticky rice. Up in the hills, the cool temperatures are per-

fect for fruit and vegetables—strawberries, apples, cabbages, mushrooms, cauliflowers, carrots and broccoli. Visit one of the fresh markets in the north and look at the profusion. Then order a gaeng kae (spicy northern-style vegetable soup). In the past, it was made with the local vegetables peculiar to the northern region. Now you will find other types of vegetables in this curry too. Another great northern vegetarian dish is tam ma-khue yao (spicy eggplant salad).

Fresh food is best. But some food also has to be stored. The northerners make several types of delicious sausage and prepared pork. Try a yam moo yor (spicy northern-style pork sausage salad).

Up in the hills, there are many different people like the Hmong, Yao, Lisu, Chinese Hor and Tai Yai. Many famous northern dishes have been adapted from their special types of cooking. Take the khao-soi noodles which are a favorite in the Lanna capital of Chiang Mai. This originated from the Chinese Hor who made their own noodles out of rice flour, and then ate them with a northern style curry instead of the usual clear soup. The result is wonderful. There's also the khanom jeen nam ngeow (Chinese spaghetti with spare ribs soup) which is even more of a confusion of cultures. Although called 'jeen' for 'Chinese', these noodles were originally eaten by the Mon in southern Burma. The sauce, 'nam', originated with the Shan, who called themselves 'ngeow'. The Shan also introduced the snack called gra-bong which is famous in the hill town of Mae Hong Sorn. Many other dishes, including the nam prik ong chilli dip, originally came from nearby Burma.

Now that you have a full stomach, it's time to explore. Northern towns have many old and distinctive temples that are worth the visit. But if you want a real adventure, go up into the hills and ride an elephant. There is no better way to experience the special ambience of the forest and the hill peoples' villages.

Luckily, the northerners make much more than food, so there are gorgeous things to buy as souvenirs. Wood carvings, lacquerware, silverware and the famous Chiang Mai umbrellas. But you can also take some Lanna food back too. The chilli dips, sausages, preserved pork and pickled garlic are all available in modern packaging. Also preserved fruit such as bale fruit, Chinese pears, sweet Chinese apricots or salty Chinese apricots. The choices are plentiful. Many are made on the Royal Project, started by His Majesty the King to find alternatives to growing opium. Buy here and you will also be contributing to a worthy cause.

Before you leave, look up again at the mists over the hills. The north is the coolest region of Thailand, but somehow it offers the warmest welcome. ■

The Northeast : Spicy Esarn

The sound of the kaen wafts across the dusty fields of Esarn, the northeastern region. The kaen is a set of pipes made from bamboo, with a plaintive tone which seems to protest against the harsh environment. At the heart of Esarn is Tung Kula Rong Hai, a desert region whose name means: even the Kula (a hardy tribe) have to cry when they cross it. But the northeasterners have learnt to smile a broad smile in the face of adversity.

The sound of the kaen is very distinctive—clear and sincere, like the Esarn people and like their food. Both the ingredients and the methods of preparation are simple. Northeasterners value nothing more than siew (friends), and always share their food even when there is not much to share.

Esarn is a high plateau. The rainfall is low and the porous soil won't hold it. Summers are diabolically hotter and longer than in other regions. But the rivers Moon and Chi support the rice and fish which all Thais rely on. The northeasterners have become expert at preserving fish

to last them through the long dry season. This pla ra, pla som or pla daek is the most distinctive feature of northeastern food.

The Moon and Chi Rivers supply the little fish. Deposits of rock salt provide the means for preserving them. The Laos call it pla daek—'stuffed fish'—because the fish and salt are stuffed into jars.

Pla ra is used for seasoning various curry paste soups, or made into the Esarn version of a chilli dip, known as jaew. You can make this yourself. First crush some chillies, garlic and salt. Then add pla ra and lime juice. You can be more adventurous by making fish, shrimp, mushroom or crayfish jaew.

Along with the saltiness of pla ra, the taste of Esarn food mixes spiciness from chillies, and sourness from tamarind juice, makok (a sort of olive), and red ants eggs. Many vegetables are special to the region. Unripe young jackfruit is boiled and eaten with chilli dip or made into soup kanoon (spicy jackfruit salad). Chaplu (wild pepper leaves) can be chopped up and added too. The region's special small and narrow bamboo shoots have to be grilled, peeled and then boiled for adding to all kinds of curries.

For Esarn people, life is a struggle. You can hear that in the sound of the kaen. They have a reputation for eating anything which will give them some scarce protein—frogs, crabs, fish, mice, snakes, birds and insects. Many kinds of insects are very popular—buffalo dung beetles, june beetles, crickets and locusts. Silkworms, which have been boiled to remove the silk and then roasted, are something of a local delicacy.

Esarn's best-known dish is som tam (spicy green papaya salad) which has now spread throughout Thailand and the world. The base is papaya, which is such a hardy tree that it grows almost anywhere. Westerners take to som tam easily because it is just like a salad. But you don't have to make som tam with papaya. Try using melon, cucumbers (northeasterners use the big cucumber called taeng larn), green bananas, or jackfruit.

Like all Thais, northeasterners eat rice but nearly always the sticky or glutinous kind. They serve it not in a plate or bowl but in a basket called a kratip. Just take a small handful of sticky rice from the kratip and roll it gently in your fingers to make a spongy ball. Then dip it in the jaew hon (northern-style spicy soup), larb esarn (spicy northeastern-style minced pork salad) or pla goong (spicy prawn salad with lemongrass). Notice that most Esarn dishes are juicy so that the liquid is easily absorbed by the sticky rice.

Sticky rice is more than a food. It's also a cultural emblem. At the annual Pee Ta Kone mask festival, the kratip baskets are made into puppet monsters and ghosts who call on the spirits for the rains to come early and swell the rice crop.

Normally Esarn people don't eat beef, because cattle and buffaloes are too few and too important for farming. But once or twice a year at festivals, they do eat beef and then they eat every part. The good meat is grilled so the drops of fat sizzle on the red-hot charcoal, then sliced into small pieces and eaten with jaew. The innards are boiled with galangal, lemongrass and kaffir lime leaves and seasoned with chillies and limes. Or made into tom krueng nai (beef offal soup), the great Esarn soup.

Anything left is minced, seasoned and made into Esarn sausages. The mixture is stuffed into casing made with intestines and left to ferment in the sun for a couple of days to get the distinctive, slightly sour taste.

The Esarn people have become great travellers. They go all over Thailand and abroad to look for work. Their food has travelled with them, so now som tam, grilled chicken, grilled pork, jaew and Esarn sausage can be found outside the region. But still the visitor can find a lot to enjoy by visiting Esarn. Choose the cool season if you can, or the rainy season when Esarn is transformed from brown to green. Visit the thousand-year-old Khmer temples and monuments which are scattered throughout the region. The best are at Phimai near Korat and at Phanom Roong in Buriram district.

Try to go at festival time and take part in a pa kao laeng. The pa kao is a table for a shared meal, just like the kuntoke from the north and the gub kao from the central plains. Usually it is made from bamboo or rattan. All the dishes are placed on the pa kao, and everyone sits round and shares. Join in and you too become one of the siew (friends).

Before saying goodbye to your Esarn friends, find something to take back home. Maybe the Esarn sausages or preserved pork like moo yor and moo yong. Perhaps a pot of jaew. If you visit the Khmer temple at Phimai, buy some of the famous Korat noodles. If you want cloth, there is plenty of cotton still handwoven in the Esarn villages and often dyed with local natural dyes. Or the beautiful sparkling colours of the silk from Chaiyaphum district

Yes, life is a struggle in the blistering heat. But nothing can be done about it, so why be miserable? The people of Esarn live each day by this motto. That's why the music of the kaen is heard constantly, both to bring joy to the northeasterners themselves, and to welcome visitors with a big smile. ■

The Central Plains: Nature's Abundance

The central plains is a great river delta. Water is everywhere, and something is always green the whole year round. The waterways used to be the highways. Still today you can paddle along one of the rivers or klongs (canals) to a floating market, a genuine Thai sight. The most famous is at Dumnern Saduak, just to the west of Bangkok. But there are many others. And all are piled high with the fresh produce of this fertile region.

This freshness and abundance is key to the region's cuisine. The preparations can be quite simple because the secret lies in the ingredients. Vegetables from the gardens. Fruit from the orchards. Fish from the rivers and canals. And of course rice from the paddy fields.

But to bring out the natural flavours, the central Thai find there is nothing to compete with a chilli dip. The sound of mortar and pestle resounds from every kitchen.

History tells us that chilli dips made with shrimp paste have been around since the time of King Narai in the 17th century. Though they are certainly spicy hot, there are many other things which make up the flavour—mango, eggplant, bale fruit—whatever takes your fancy.

For dipping, Thais use whatever vegetables are in season, fresh and cheap. Cucumbers, morning glory stalks, makok leaves, cha-om and gratin. Many can just be collected along the hedgerows.

Besides being a central dish in its own rice, chilli paste dip is at the heart of many more complex dishes. The yam or spicy Thai salad is one such development. Besides the spiciness, a good yam should have a great aroma from kaffir lime leaves, lemongrass and other herbs. Many local vegetables can be made into yum such as yam tua phu (spicy winged bean salad), and yam hua plee (spicy banana bud salad). The gaeng liang (spicy mixed vegetable soup) is also developed from fish paste, boiled with water to make a soup, and filled with tum lueng, gourds, and other vegetables which grow along garden fences. Delicious and healthy too.

The secret of making a good gaeng curry lies in the way you mix and balance the ingredients. Chillies, onions, garlic, galangal, lemongrass, coriander roots, kaffir lime zest and shrimp paste are the staples, but there are many variations. It's important that all are finely ground and well mixed together so that the taste suffuses through the vegetables, fish and meat.

Don't believe that all Thai dishes have to be very spicy hot. Many are rather mild. Look in a central plains village and you will find all the houses are on stilts. This is both to escape the floods, and to make a space for keeping animals. Most houses have a coop there for chickens and ducks. Eggs are an everyday food— boiled, fried or steamed. Omelette is a constant standby. Son-in-law eggs are a favorite with both adults and children. And if you must still have them spicy hot, then you can always make fried or hard-boiled eggs into a yam.

The central plains also has its version of som tam (spicy green papaya salad). Compared to the Esarn som tam, it's sweeter, sourer, not so spicy, and has ground peanuts for a crunchy texture. Generally the food in the central region is sweeter than in other regions. But not every dish.

Let's go back to the garden fence. It's not only the vegetables growing there that can be eaten. Many of the flowers are eaten too. You can make a yam with roses. Other flowers can be mixed in a gaeng som, eaten alongside kanom jeen nam phrik, or simply just stir-fried. Some favourites are the flower of the banana and the khilek tree.

For centuries the capital has been in this central region. Civil servants used to send their daughters to live in the capital to learn the arts of cooking, carving fruit, making embroidery and arranging flowers. Often the dishes of the central region have a sumptuous elegance which has been influenced by the intricate traditions of the palace kitchens.

A wonderful example is khao chae (summer time rice), a dish specially for the hot months of the summer. Preparation has to begin at least a day in advance. The water must be scented by steeping flowers. Choose the flowers that will bloom overnight. If you are using jasmine, nip out the stem because this will make the water cloudy. Steep the flowers for 4-5 hours and then remove. Leave the water overnight with a scented candle burning. To serve, add boiled rice and ice to the water, and serve alongside little balls of fried shrimp paste, shredded beef, stuffed paprika, and fresh carved vegetables such as ginger and cucumber. This dish is a perfect refresher for the humid weather.

And so to the dessert. This region has many types but most are made with only three basic ingredients—flour, coconut and sugar. Somehow Thai cooks boil, preserve, stir, fry, steam and mix these three ingredients into all kinds of shapes and flavours such as piak poon, kanom sord sai, kanom tuay, and kanom tong dang tom kao.

Marie Guimar, wife of the 17th-century Greek adventurer, Constantine Phaulkon, introduced a fourth ingredient—eggs. Many desserts have a Thai-European flavour such as tong yip, tong yord, foy tong and sang khaya.

Central Thais like to enhance the colour of foods using natural dyes. Green comes from pandan leaves, yellow from turmeric, red from lac, blue from butterfly peas, and black from coconut husks which have been fired then steeped in water. All these dyes are totally natural and non-chemical.

For another dessert, the region's abundant fruits can be eaten on their own, or made into loy gaew with ice and syrup. And because so much fruit is available, central Thais have become expert at preserving them so they don't go to waste.

All the chopping, pounding and mixing in central-plains cooking can seem quite tedious. But it has always been very much a family affair, something which bound the family together. Little girls help their mums and grandmothers to wash the vegetables, peel the onions and split the garlic. Elder sister slices up pork and makes coconut milk. Son is asked by his mother to chop the pork and to show his form with mortar and pestle. Then as the sun sinks and the evening breezes blow along the klong, mother sets up the mats and tables on the terrace so that the family can gather round, partake in the natural abundance of their environment, and enjoy the closeness of kin and friends — as Thais have done for centuries. ■

Bangkok: Hurry up!

I f we were a bird flying over Bangkok, it would look similar to other capital cities throughout the world. It is the center of development, trade, and business in Thailand, where people of all types migrate towards the tall corporate buildings, and the small family-owned shop houses.

The morning sun doesn't rise from the hills or woods, but it slowly inches its way up between the buildings that tower in the sky, marking the beginning of a new day... Wake up, Bangkok!

Now, as we glide over the city and get ready to land, the people of Bangkok prepare the colorful and delectable variety of food that is offered at any time of the day. At the crack of dawn, people are already in a hurry. In order to arrive at work on time, many people will stop at one of thousands of food stalls that are located on every street throughout the city. These food stalls offer delicious recipes from pa tong go (deep-fried twin dough) , salapao (Chinese steamed buns), and kanom krok (coconut pudding). They can be thoroughly enjoyed with fresh coffee, tea, milk, or soybean milk.

If one has a larger appetite, they can have a bowl of hot jok moo (pork congee), or a small bowl of rice with hot, clear soup. After their stomach is full, they can tackle the work at the office.

N oon. Lunch time offers a wide selection of food to choose from, differing in taste, style, and cultural background. Typically, lunch is cheap and will include a wide variety of delicious seasonings.

Rice is the Thai staple food. If you enjoy rice, then the quick menu will offer you many popular dishes, including fried rice. This rice is fried in a pan, and can include pork, chicken, prawns, or squid. Onions and tomatoes are added, followed by light seasonings such as fish sauce. This dish is quick and convenient which must be served hot. The fried rice can further be adjusted to make khao ga-phrao moo khai dao (fried red basil pork and fried egg with rice), where more tantalizing spices are included, such as chilli and garlic.

A special herb in this quick dish is red basil, in which the smell and taste can be revitalizing. People in India believe that these are sacred trees, as they plant them in their homes to avoid going to hell. When the leaves are crushed, the smell helps to eliminate the affects of dizziness or influenza. Other quick rice dishes are kao man gai (steamed chicken rice), kao nar ped, kao kar moo, and kao with gaeng. Each offers distinctive tastes and styles. Next to the rice stall is a vending cart selling noodles. The huge noodle bowl is filled with boiling hot soup that penetrates the noses of people walking by. The glass shelf next to the bowl contains many different types of tempting meatballs, such as fish balls, shrimp balls, pork balls, or seaweed meatballs. In the small bowl, there are soft and braised chicken legs.

It is said that the Chinese invented noodles. This culinary culture spread throughout Southeast Asia by the Hokien and Kwang Toong Chinese who immigrated to Thailand during the 15th century. Many of the lightweight, plastic tables and chairs seen at noodle stands across Bangkok were brought by the Chinese since they can be carried around very easily.

The white strands of noodles come in three sizes: small, medium, and large. Thai people began adding these Chinese noodles to a much larger variety of recipes. They make a quick and healthy lunch. They can be boiled, stir-fried, or deep-fried. They can be served in water or without water, but the most important thing is how they are seasoned.

The most popular type of noodles is guay teow nam moo (rice noodles with pork soup). An extremely important ingredient is the soup that the noodles are served in. The soup is boiled and simmered in pork bones that make the noodles smell irresistible. Dry noodles without soup are best with fried garlic. Another guay teow moo is the yen ta fo (rice noodles in red soup) which uses morning glories to layer the bowl instead of bean sprouts. The ingredients in Yen Ta Fo include fried squid, tofu, and pork blood. Certain types of red sauce can be used to season it. Finally, many years ago, guay teow lord (flat rice noodles with minced pork) had tiny shrimp that were tucked into the noodle flour. Today, the flour is used as a wrapper for the ingredients, which include boiled bean sprouts, tofu, three layered pork, and drops of sweet soya sauce which is later added.

The first quick Thai dish that foreign visitors may want to start with is phad Thai (fried rice noodles). Although the name of this dish sounds Thai, it is believed that this dish originated in China since many of the ingredients are similar to the noodles. The difference is that phad Thai is fried in a pan. When eating noodles, you must not forget the condiment tray. This tray includes small bowls of sugar, fish sauce, ground pepper, and crushed nuts. Some restaurants will include small servings of vegetables or bean sprouts as a side dish.

Although times change, the fun of creating new exciting dishes still remains with the Thais. Bangkok Thais pay particular attention to literature and the arts, and one unusual dish arising from the Thai version of the classical epic, the Ramayana, is pra ram long song (steamed morning glory with sauteed red curry). The Thai folk hero of this epic is Pra Ram, whose entire body was green. In this dish, he is represented by the bright green morning glory leaves, while the curry paste soup of chicken, prawns, and spices represents the golden pond he bathed in.

Lunch is over, and it now appears to be approaching late afternoon since your stomach is growling for some more delicious food. What will you eat for a snack? One popular Thai snack is kao tung nar tung. This recipe was invented from leftovers. Many years ago, Thais used to cook rice in a huge, family-sized bowl which meant that there would be leftover rice that could be eaten later. Instead of disposing of the rice, first it was dried under the sun, and then deep-fried. These were then eaten as various snacks—kao tung nar tung, kao tung mieng lao, and kao tung nar maprao. Kao tung is now usually cooked in an oven to make it crispy. Kao tung can then be dipped into nar tung, which is a salty and creamy sauce.

A popular noodle dish is made up of yellow noodles and wontons. Like other noodles, these are sold throughout the day, but they are most popular in the evenings and late at night in Bangkok. Usually, a noodle vendor will wander

through the streets tapping two wooden sticks against his cart. This signals to the neighborhood that the noodle vendor has arrived.

In the evenings in Bangkok, the taste of Thai food is incredible. But, like other large cities, the traffic in Bangkok is horrendous and prevents many people from dining in exquisite restaurants since they are exhausted from work. Luckily, there are many fresh markets selling prepared and cooked food that can be taken straight home to enjoy. Some of these choices include hot curry, clear soup, spicy soup, stir-fried vegetables, fried pork, and grilled chicken. The more adventurous person can stroll around the market and gather fresh ingredients to cook something back home. If you would like to enjoy some soup, get some chicken and a few gourds, and braise with mushrooms. But, if you don't want anything too difficult, try this khao khai jeow moo sab (minced pork omelets with rice). All you need are a few eggs, beaten with minced pork and fish sauce. Pour this mixture into a pan with hot oil. When the mixture becomes yellow and crispy, just set it on top of a hot plate of rice and you will have a simple, yet delicious meal.

No matter how late it is, Bangkok never sleeps! If you become hungry in the middle of the night, there are night markets located all over the city. These open early in the evening and close at dusk. The selection is endless. You can choose from many favorite Thai foods including fried mussels, fish congee, guay teow with soup, bread and sangkhaya, bua loy kai warn, and potatoes boiled in ginger.

As times change with the rush and diversity of Bangkok, Thai cuisine provides an exciting array of foods from many cultures blended together into one. ■

The Gulf of Thailand:
Relax and Indulge by the Seaside

The coasts of the Gulf of Thailand are dotted with little ports and fishing villages which have a very special charm all of their own. Some have now become resorts, such as Bang Saen and Pattaya, where westerners like to enjoy the sun, sand and sea. But for the Thais, a visit to the seaside is about one thing: food. Pay a visit to Bang Saen, the resort which is closest to Bangkok. The beachfront is lined with eating stalls. On a weekend, these are packed with Bangkok people enjoying a break and an enormous meal.

This is not surprising, because the Gulf of Thailand still gives a varied harvest of splendid seafood—shrimps, molluscs, crabs and fish. Fish include pla jaramed, pla kapong, pla insi and groupers. No matter how you prepare them, they will always be wonderful if you eat them fresh. You can barbecue, grill or steam them and dip them in fish sauce produced locally.

But to get the real value of Thai seafood, you need to try the dishes made in a characteristic Thai way. Prawns are prawns, but tom yam goong (spicy prawn soup) is a dish which has made Thai cooking famous throughout the world.

Many foreigners don't realise that there are many subtle varieties of tom yam goong. Some are hotter. Some use more lime or more lemongrass. Some add more fish sauce. Some of the variation depends on the locality. But a lot more simply depends on the cook. An old-fashioned housewife will shake her head and tell you that there are no exact measurements in cooking. It is all about creating your own taste, changing it however you want to, suiting the Thai saying that "to do whatever your heart desires is to be truly Thai". The fact that there are no exact recipes is one of the main charms of Thai cooking. There is no need to know how many tablespoons of fish sauce you will need, how much tamarind juice or shrimp paste. Because the ingredients are natural, they themselves vary. Tamarinds, for example, differ in size, and if coming from different places, might not even taste the same. In the old days, Thais recorded measurements with parts of the body—a fist of this, a thumb of that, a pinch or handful of the other. Thai cooks know that the cook's skill lies in the taste buds, not in the measurements.

One seafood dish with an amusing name is poh taek. When fishermen return from sea, their poh (fishing boat) is crammed with a wealth of sea life such as shrimps, molluscs, crabs and fish. Imagine what would happen should the poh (boat) taek (explode)! The result would be the tom yam poh taek (exploded boat), with every kind of seafood mixed in the fiery flavour of a tom yam.

This is one version of a Thai minestrone. Another very different version is tom som pla too, an orange curry made with the local variety of mackerel. A good tom som should have a sour taste from tamarind juice, a sweet taste from the sugarcane placed at the bottom of the bowl, spiciness from the pepper and fresh ginger, and a heavenly aroma from the garnish of spring onions.

The coast on the east side of the Gulf is the home of many special dishes. Chantaburi province down close to the Cambodian border produces its own local noodles which are soft and chewy. They are great for making fried guay teow with chunks of crab meat, and they are a good choice for phad Thai (fried rice noodles). This area is also the only place where you can find the chamuang leaves which go into gaeng moo chamuang . The tree grows only in the forests close to the Gulf around Chantaburi and the neighbouring districts of Rayong and Trat. Chantaburi people say that this dish has to be reduced over low heat for a very long time, preferably overnight, so that the soup will saturate the meat and give the correct rich and spicy flavour.

This eastern part also has its own chilli paste dip, nam phrik khai poo, made with crab's eggs and yellow chillies which give it a great spicy flavour as well as enticing color.

Another seafood dish which is found all along the Gulf is hor mok. Curry paste, fish and coconut milk are mixed together and put in banana leaf containers and steamed. Or the mixture can be grilled to produce the slightly different dish called ngop. Nowadays, hor mok is often made in coconut shells rather than the traditional banana leaf. You can make it with fish alone, or with a mixture of all kinds of seafood.

But not all the food on the Gulf has to be seafood. Yam yai contains a bit of everything. Put it in a large plate. Season with a bit of Japanese fish sauce. Oh it smells divine.

All the countries in the region have some kind of spicy salad which the Thais call yam. Traditionally they are supposed to combine five tastes which can be counted on the fingers of the hand. The Burmese word for this kind of dish, laytok, literally means seasoning with the hand. Sourness should come first, then sweetness, saltiness and spiciness. The fifth taste is the central ingredient of the yam, and for Thais almost anything can be made into a yam—meat, fish, vegetables, flowers or fruit.

Yam yai just means big yam, and it can have a bit of everything. The distinctive taste comes from Japanese-style fish sauce, which became popular in Siam from the early 19th century. Now there are fish sauce factories all along the Gulf. It's easy to make when the sea has so much fish, the coasts are lined with salt-pans, and the hot temperature facilitates fermentation. The best quality fish sauce

should be used to make nam jim rot ded (delicious sauce) which is the perfect accompaniment for seafood that is either barbecued or grilled.

If you are looking for a souvenir to take back home from the Gulf, pay a visit to Nong Mon market in Chonburi province to the east of Bangkok. There you can enjoy the dessert known as khao larm. In the past, travellers packed rice into a hollow bamboo. This later became transformed into a dessert. Sticky rice is mixed with coconut milk and sugar, packed in a bamboo tube, and cooked over a fire. Thai holiday-makers like to stop off at Nong Mon to buy some khao larm to take home.

But Nong Mon has much more than this. There are piles of dried seafood such as squid, shrimps and pla kem (salted fish), which make good gifts for friends and your loved ones. Then in the hot season there is stall after stall groaning with durians, rambutans, mangosteens, rakam and custard apples.

There's no doubt that if you visit the coast of the Gulf of Thailand, you will end up spending much of your holiday just like a Thai—eating! The beaches are lovely, but the seafood is simply irresistible. ■

The South : the Fiery Charm of the South

The humid wind from the rubber plantation. The distant scent of the Andaman Sea. A sacred Muslim song, the Amman, rising into the air, backed by the distinctive sound of a manora-sop band. The charm of Thailand's south is very special.

Thailand is shaped like an old-fashioned axe. The narrow handle running down between the Gulf of Thailand and the Andaman Sea, connects the Thai heartland to the Malaysian Peninsula. The monsoon winds from the sea and Muslim influences from the south combine to create the specialness of this regional cuisine.

Thais of all regions 'gin khao gin pla' (eat fish eat rice). But the narrow hilly peninsula of the south has little room for growing rice, while the sea is never very far away, and still relatively abundant. The south's cuisine is more fish than rice.

The fishing boats leave in the early evening and return at dawn, bringing back a wealth of prawns, molluscs, crabs and fish. Just boiling, grilling or barbecuing transforms them into a delicious meal. But southerners like to season them in their own distinctive style, such as goong gathi nor mai sod (prawn and bamboo shoot in coconut soup), poo phad phong garee (fried yellow curry crab), goong phad sator (fried prawn with twisted cluster beans), and gaeng lueng (spicy coconut shoot soup). Many of these dishes have a yellow colour from turmeric. It adds its own pleasant aroma similar to galangal while helping to kill the smell of fish and other seafood.

Another distinctive flavour is added by koei, the southern variant of shrimp paste. It's made with the small shrimps caught in the dragnets but too small for sale. Southerners like to eat as much of the fish as possible, especially the maw, and the spicy gaeng tai pla is one of the region's most famous dishes.

The sea coasts are fringed with coconut trees so it's no surprise that coconut is a staple of southern cooking. Gaeng lueng yod maphrao (spicy coconut shoot soup) is made from coconuts, coconut shoots, and coconut milk. The gratai (rabbit) coconut scraper comes from the genius of this region. What other kitchen utensils have been designed to sit on?

Mussamun my darling. You smell of coriander, so fiery.
Any man who gets to taste the soup will dream of you.

"Mussamun" comes from the old word for Muslim, and this unique curry arrived in the south along the trade routes that range from Arabia through India. The basic ingredients in southern curries are the same as those found in other regions—chilli, onion, garlic, galangal, lemongrass, coriander roots, kaffir lime zest and shrimp paste. But southerners give more prominence to the five powdered spices. This is an Indian influence. And when you taste a mussamun beef or chicken curry, you can trace this origin.

The southern curries have a reputation for being very hot. The southern gaeng som is hot and sour. Gaeng tai pla is hot and salty. Why do the southern people have a taste for such food? They cannot really explain it. They just know that the tingling feeling on the tongue is very satisfying. Also, some attribute it to the climate. The region is always humid and people get sick easily. They believe that

hot food makes them sweat, and this helps to ward off fevers.

To temper the spiciness of their curries, southerners eat them with lots of fresh, pickled or boiled vegetables to ease the burning tongue. Twisted cluster beans are a favorite of the south, especially in goong phad sator (fried prawn with twisted cluster beans) or sweet and sour twisted cluster beans.

Another regional dish with lots of vegetables is khao yam, made with grated coconut and a special dressing made from the koei shrimp paste.

The cultural background of the south is very varied. For centuries, the region has been a stopping place on the sea routes from east to west. Visitors came from China, from India, from Arabia, and from Java. The four southernmost provinces of Satun, Naratthiwat, Pattani and Yala have their own Muslim community. Many of the other towns have a lot of Fujian Chinese. If you visit Phuket, look out for their unusual houses. Many southern dishes have a trace of Fujian cuisine.

An example is dub tay or jub tee, which is shortened from the Chinese name of lum dub lon gnai tee.

The Muslim and Chinese influences on southern food are often quite opposite. The Muslim food tends to be aromatic, spicy and highly coloured. Take the Muslim fast-food favorite, khao mok gai, which is yellow, or the fried chicken eaten with sticky rice sprinkled with fried onion or fried garlic. By contrast the Chinese dishes are blander both in taste and appearance. While you are in Phuket, make sure you try the Phuket Hokkien (Fujian) noodles—soft noodles fried and seasoned with a characteristic Chinese sauce.

In fact Phuket has a lot of its own local dishes. Another noodle variety is mee sapam. And Phuket has its own contribution to the array of chilli paste dips in nam phrik goong siap which is made from grilled shrimps. Make sure you finish off your Phuket meal with the Phuket pineapple. They are smaller, crisper and sweeter than the usual variety, and Phuket people are rightly proud of them. You can see the pineapple plantations all over the island.

But pineapples are not the only southern fruit. The climate is especially good for fruit-growing and there are fruit available in every season. Try the delicious scented white flesh of the mangosteens, or the delicate flavour of longan, or the rich splendour of a durian. If you happen to be visiting this province during the tenth lunar month, you will see Phuket's colourful festival. People visit the temples with offerings to pay respect to their deceased relatives.

Before you return, make sure you buy some of the local foods to take back with you along with memories. The region has lots of dried seafood preparations including dried shrimp, dried squid, and dried fish. Then there are bottles of the region's koei fish paste, and some special types of pickled fish. If you still have room left in your bag, treat yourself to some of the handicrafts, such as the leather puppets used in the region's famous puppet dramas, or the silver, silk, sarongs and batik which all show evidence of the south's Malay influences.

Whatever you buy, you will be sure to take back the memory of the spicy-hot southern cuisine. Once tasted, it is quite unforgettable. ▪

Life and Rice

Thais don't say they "dine", they say they "pai kin khao", literally "go to eat rice." The word "khao" in the Thai mind means both rice and food, even if the meal doesn't include rice. It is sometimes difficult for the non-Thai to understand the importance attached to food and eating in Thai society. Nearly all social occasions involve eating. Food is a major topic of conversation. And snacking is so popular that Thais sometimes seem to be eating all the time.

For centuries, rice has played an important part in Thai culture. Although modernization has affected some traditions, rice still plays a central role in Thai people's lives. The traditional way of cooking rice is still the favorite method. After eating, those who appreciate the gift of food put their hands together to thank the rice seedlings for filling their stomachs. Someone who has carelessly dropped grains of rice on the floor will ask for the forgiveness of Mae Phosop (the goddess of rice). The whiteness of rice is often compared to the purity of Buddhism. There is a close relationship between the Thais and every single grain of rice. It has been that way ever since "The Tale of the Rain" began.

A Tale of the Rain

May heralds the summer rains... The first drops of rain splatter onto the earth. The calendar says May. All the young boys and girls rejoice in the coming of the first rain. It means the fierce dry season is passing. Work in the rice-fields will soon begin.

When the sun rises above the horizon, the farmers take out their 'iron buffaloes' for the first 2-3 rounds of plowing. Some use just a hoe for the customary 'first plowing', choosing a Monday or Friday as these days are considered auspicious for this event.

Ai Tui and Ee Puek, the real buffaloes, are summoned out to the paddy-fields to trample the grass and stubble into the ground to work as a fertilizer. Once this is done, the seedbeds are ready for planting. The rice seeds are soaked in water for 2-3 days until little white shoots appear, and then sown in the seedbed. A month later the green shoots ripple in the summer breezes, bringing hope to those who have put so much work into them.

The main fields still have to be prepared for transplanting the seedlings. The father and his eldest son, the power-houses of the family, start plowing the land before break of dawn. They rest only when they hear either mother or daughter arrive with the traditional Thai bento and call out the magic words 'time for lunch!'

The young kids who are not yet ready for the hard work take the buffaloes to graze along the banks of the paddy-fields. After lunch, work resumes as usual until sun down.

Some fields are far away from home. The men set out with the buffaloes before dawn. The bells around the animals' necks wake up the children and the old people who stay behind. By the field, they build a shack for shelter from the mid-day sun. Each day the work is back-breaking. Relief comes only on festival days, when they stop work to give alms to the monks.

The rice seedlings sway bravely in the gusty winds of July. Now the women of the family play their part. They gather the seedlings in bunches and plunge them into the main field, now fully plowed and calf-deep in water. Everyone in the family plays a part, so all in the family may have enough to eat. Before long, the fields are done and the plowing season is over.

Goddess of Rice : Three to four months after transplanting, an ear appears on each rice stalk. The grains start to form from a milky-white liquid called 'rice milk'. A green topshoot encases and protects the young grain.

Now the rice is said to be 'pregnant', just like a woman ready to give birth. For centuries, Thais have believed that there is a guardian spirit, Mother Phosop, who exists in every single stalk of rice. If she is looked after well, she will make the fields fertile and abundant. So when the rice plants are pregnant, so too is Mother Phosop.

Rice is not the only thing to have a guardian spirit. One exists in every living thing including humans, cows and buffaloes. If someone falls ill, it shows the guardian spirit has gone away somewhere. Family and friends hold a ceremony to call the spirit back. In the north of Thailand, when the fields have been prepared, villagers hold a ceremony to thank the spirits of the cattle and buffaloes for their hard work, and to apologise if they hit them or drove them too hard.

"Dearest, sweetest Mother. Come and stay with us. Come and look after our children and grandchildren. Come and accept these offerings of food. They will ease your morning sickness. Come and receive our gifts of rice from the north and salt from the south. Take these children and grandchildren under your loving care."

The songs of the people calling out to Mother Phosop to accept their offerings echo around the field. A bunch of bananas, a coconut, an orange and a red-and-white Thai dessert are set out on trays or banana-leaves decorated with red and white paper. Sometimes the women make a lattice basket for Mother Phosop and fill it with betel, chewing tobacco, bananas, sugarcane and sour fruit. The basket is hung in the middle of the field. Some try even harder to please Mother Phosop. They persuade a young woman to offer her comb, vanity mirror, silk shawl and other beauty accessories.

After this, farmers regularly do the round of their fields to check that rats are not destroying the plants. Sometimes they put up scarecrows to fool the pests that there is someone constantly on guard. Scarecrows are believed to have another purpose: if there is a disease going around, the scarecrows will catch it rather than the villagers.

At last the rice-fields are brushed by cooler breezes. By now the green expanse has turned into a sea of gold. For a farmer and his family, there is no sight more beautiful.

The golden grains are collected in baskets. The farmers carry them on their heads to store in the granary. Harvest is a time for singing. Friends and families help one another to complete the task before a sudden rainstorm can arrive and ruin the crop. This is a time for getting together. Many new couples are made during the harvest time. Before anyone knows it, the work is complete.

But first the rice has to be threshed and divided up—one part for eating, the other to sell. The cut stalks are piled in the yard. Ai Tui and Ee Puek, the buffaloes, are called on again to thresh the grains by trampling. Before storing, the granary must first be blessed. Only women can do this. Once, Mother Phosop appeared and a man was so struck by her beauty that he tried to rape her. Since then she has never appeared again. ■

Mae Phosop

A long time ago, there was a goddess called Mother Phosop who wished to be born as a grain of rice so that she could feed mankind. With the help of a hermit, her wish came true.

Back then, rice was like a human—it had a heart and a soul. But, unlike a human, it could also fly. At the proper season, rice would fly into the granaries for people to eat.

Then one day, everything changed. A widow failed to complete building her granary on time. When the rice flew up to the granary along with Mother Phosop, the widow was confused. She took up a pole and chased them away. Mother Phosop was very hurt, and went off to live in the Himapan forest in the distant mountains.

The people had no food. Everyone suffered. Some died of hunger. In desperation, a hermit volunteered to go and plead for Mother Phosop to return. At first, she refused, saying how cruel human beings were. But eventually she gave in. She decided to hold her breath until she died and was reborn as a grain of rice. The hermit returned to his people and gave them the rice seed to plant and propagate. From that day onwards, mankind has treated rice with great respect. Farmers ask Mother Phosop for permission before planting her seeds, before transplanting, before harvest, before threshing, and before pounding. When the season is over and the rice is safely stored in the granary, they hold a ceremony to thank Mother Phosop for her sacrifice and her bounty. ■

Buddhism

The sound of the cock's crow resonates across the village. The great orange sun announces the dawn. Over nearly every household, a plume of smoke rises from the kitchen as housewives hasten to cook the rice for giving as alms to the monks. Villagers wait in front of their houses with offerings of food, flowers, joss sticks and candles for the line of monks making their way up the street. Those with homes along the river wait at the river's edge for the monks who paddle along in their boat.

These sights recur every day— except during Buddhist Lent which falls in the rainy season. Everyone is too busy. The rice plants are just beginning to sprout. According to legend, some monks once trod carelessly on the precious young crop. Villagers were angry. So the Buddha ordered that in this season the monks should stay in the temple and engage in study and meditation— until the rains pass and the rice is ready for harvest.

There is another story about rice among the stories about the life of the Buddha. In the Himapan forest, the Buddha was meditating under a Bo tree by a stream. A pregnant maiden prayed to the tree spirit to give her a son, in return for which she would offer the spirit a bowl of magic rice porridge. When her wish came true, she took milk from 1000 cows and fed it to 500 cows, which produced milk which was fed to 250, and so on down to a final 8 cows whose extra rich and creamy milk was used to make the magic porridge. The maiden mistook the Buddha for the tree spirit, and offered him the porridge in a golden bowl. The Buddha decided to taste it. He reflected that he had been six years in the forest, meditating in search of enlightenment. He decided to leave the forest. He put his spirit in the golden bowl and floated it on the stream. He prayed that if he truly discovered truth, let this golden bowl flow against the current. And the miracle happened... ■

Thailand is the world's rice-bowl. Thailand's paddy-fields not only feed the nation's people but also bring an immense amount of income into the country. Thailand is the world's largest rice-exporter, and the home of the fragrant or jasmine rice which is loved for its aroma, softness and taste. The rice-farmers are the backbone of the country and, with the tireless support of His Majesty the King, the relationship between rice and farmers shall never fade.

"I have myself studied and experienced what it is like to be a farmer. I realise how demanding and exhausting it can be. There are so many problems to overcome."

In the 1950s, the King set up an experimental rice farm in the grounds of the Chitlada Palace in the heart of Bangkok. He pioneered the use of the motor-driven plough and closely supervised the farm's operations. On occasions he drove the tractor and planted the seedlings himself.

Ever since, samples from these experimental fields are used for the Royal Ploughing Ceremony. This auspicious ceremony dates back to the old Thai kingdom of the 13th century. It is timed before the rains come at the start of the rice-growing season. Nowadays the ceremony takes place on the Pramane ground outside Bangkok's old royal palace.

First the royal clairvoyant will carry out traditional rites for that time of year. Then the King goes to the Temple of the Emerald Buddha with rice in silver and gold containers, along with other crops such as lettuce, green beans, cucumber, corn, taro and potatoes. The King prays to the Emerald Buddha and other deities that Thailand's harvests may be abundant.

The ploughing ceremony takes place at the break of dawn, marked by the sounding of a gong. The lord of the ceremony, appointed by the King, ploughs a plot to plant the rice seeds from the gold and silver containers. He is helped by a fine team of bullocks in splendid array. The most important moment of the event comes when one bullock is allowed to choose among seven trays containing respectively rice, corn, beans, sesame, alcohol, water and grass. A priest informs the royal clairvoyant which tray the bullock chooses. The crop on the chosen tray will be particularly abundant that year. If the bullock chooses the alcohol, it means international trade will prosper.

Then one proud man is announced as the outstanding Thai farmer of the year. He is honoured to accept the award from the King, who has been watching the proceedings from a nearby marquee. After the royal anthem is played, the King takes his leave. This is a signal for farmers and other on-lookers to gather up some of the grains used in the ceremony as a blessing and as a token of hope for a prosperous year. ■

Traditional rice cooking
There are altogether four methods
Cooking wet
-Wash the rice grains.
-Place in a pot and fill with 3-4 inches of water. Place over heat and bring to the boil.
-When cooked, pour out excess water. This process is called dong kao.

Cooking dry
-Same as above but use only 1-2 inches of water.
-Boil over low heat, stirring constantly so that rice is evenly cooked.
-Cover with lid and leave on low heat until water is completely absorbed and the rice has been evenly cooked.

Steaming by pot.
-Put rice in a pot and add water about 1-1/2 inches above the level of the rice.
-Use a larger cooking pot. Add water. Place the pot with the rice inside and close the lid. Steam until done.

Steaming by huad.
- Soak the rice in cold water for 10 hours or more (or hot water for 5 hours).
- Wrap the rice in a thin cloth and place in a cooking basket or huad.
- Add water to the lower pot, place the huad above it, and bring to boil.
- The rice will be ready in 40-60 minutes or about the time it takes for a joss stick to burn down.
- In Esarn, this process is called mar kao

Nowadays electric rice-cookers make it much simpler! ■

The secret of Thai cooking lies in blending different tastes into one harmonious result. Ingredients should be the freshest possible. The experienced cook knows how to combine herbs, spices and seasonings to create the perfect balance of taste and color.

Bale Fruit (Ma-toom)

Bale fruit grows on tall trees. They are large and egg-shaped with a hard skin which turns from green to yellow when ripe. The bright orange flesh inside makes nam ma-toom (bale fruit juice) which Thais love as a thirst-quencher. The fruit has to be peeled and crushed, then boiled until the bale fruit juice suffuses the water. The juice can be enjoyed as it is, or with added sugar if you have a sweet tooth. Thai also makes a tea from dried bale fruit. Bale fruit can be diced and cooked in syrup for storing.

Banana (Gluay)

Most Thai household gardens have banana trees because the fruit are very nutritious, and almost every part of the plant has some use. Thailand has many different types of banana. Gluay narm war are small and pudgy. They are rich in minerals, calcium and vitamins. Gluay kai are smaller—finger-size—with brown spots. Many people like these best. Gluay horm are larger and similar to the bananas found in the west.

Banana leaves can be used as a cooking container for dishes like Hor Mok (Steamed Mixed Seafood Cake).

Coconut (Ma-phrao)

Coconuts will grow almost anywhere, but they like the stable temperature provided by the sea. Coconut plantations are found throughout Thailand's coasts and islands. Monkeys are trained to climb the trees and pick the coconuts. The dwarf coconut (ma-phrao ton tia) is usually picked under-ripe for the refreshing juice and delicate taste of the young flesh. The tall coconut trees are harvested when the nuts are fully ripe, and the flesh can be grated to make the coconut milk used in gaeng and various other dishes. Coconut contains a lot of saturated fat, but is less fattening than most people think because this fat burns off easily.

Custard Apple

Custard apple (Noy-nah)

Custard apples have a light green or cream-coloured, knobby skin. The Thai variety tends to be smaller than those found elsewhere. Just gently break one apart in your hands and scoop out the creamy fragrant flesh inside. The taste is sweet and rich with just a trace of sourness. They are only really good when just ripe, and go too soft and too sweet when past their prime. The season is June to September. Custard apples make a wonderful ice cream. A handful of their leaves, crushed and mixed with 1-2 tablespoons of coconut juice, can be used to kill lice. Apply the liquid onto the lice-infested head, wrap with towel and leave for about half an hour, then wash hair.

Durian

Durian (Tu-rian)

Durians are about the size of a jackfruit with large, sharp spikes. You love them or you hate them. The smell is strong and surprising—sometimes compared to ripe camembert. But the taste can be addictive. Durians should be eaten as soon as they are picked. Each durian contains two to three segments of creamy flesh round a large seed. A popular variety is mon thong (golden pillow). The flesh is firm, golden yellow, and very sweet. The aficionado's choice is kradoom thong (golden button), which are smaller and have a smoother, richer taste. Garn yao (long stem) durians are also large and have a lighter flavour.

Guava

Guava (Farang)

Thai guavas are different to the small, pink-fleshed type found elsewhere. They are large with a green skin and white flesh. Thais like to eat them rather under-ripe when the flesh is slightly sweet and very crisp. No need to peel or cut out the pips. The whole lot can be eaten. They are best with a dip of powdered chilli and salt. Chopped guava adds a bit of crunchiness to a fruit salad. Some people love them pickled. You can also make fresh guava juice by using a blender. Guavas contain vitamin C and A as well as other valuable elements which help prevent gum disease. You can also make a liquid by boiling their leaves which is good as a breath-freshener and also as a relief for skin rashes and swelling.

Jackfruit (Kha-nun)

Jackfruit are the largest fruit in the world. They have a rough, uneven, yellowish-brown skin. Inside, the flesh is divided into many small segments with a glossy soft skin. Colour and taste depend on the variety, but the most common have a rich yellow colour and a strong sweet taste. The fruit can be eaten on its own but is even better with syrup and crushed ice. In Esarn, the jackfruit is used in dishes such as jackfruit soup. The seeds can be boiled in salty water to make a snack. Thais like to grow a jackfruit tree in their garden because they believe it brings good luck. The Thai name 'kanoon' sounds very like a Thai word for support or help.

Langsat (Lang-sad)

Langsats are quite round and grow in bunches. They are yellow and their skin contains a sticky white sap. The meat has five uneven segments. They are sweet with a hint of sourness, and can be eaten fresh. The bark of the langsat tree is used to treat dysentery and scorpion stings. The seeds help to lower fever and also to get rid of intestinal worms. Another kind of fruit which closely resembles the langsat are the bigger, tastier and more expensive longgong. These are sweeter than langsats because they don't have any sap in their skin. Some say that longgongs are the best fruit after durians. Long gongs and langsats are both available in Thailand between the months of June-October.

Mango (Ma-muang)

For many the most delicious tropical fruit is the mango. Thai mangoes can be enjoyed either ripe or unripe. There are several kinds grown in Thailand and each region has its own favourite. For eating ripe, choose ok-rong, narm dork mai, or thong dum. They are excellent eaten as Khao Neow Ma-muang (Ripe Mango and Sticky Rice). They also can be made into a refreshing sorbet. For eating unripe and crispy-crunchy, choose kaew, raed, pim sane, keow sawoey, or the mun norng saeng. These are delicious with chilli powder and salt dip. Unfortunately, the mango season lasts only from February to May. But the rest of the year you can still get dried mangoes or mango paste. Mangoes are high in vitamin A. Eating the fresh skin helps to cure gum disease, relieve asthma, reduce phlegm, and combat nausea.

Mangosteen (Mang-kud)

Mangosteens are small and round with a hard skin. While ripening they are pinkish red and turn dark purple when fully ripe. Choose the fruit by pressing the skin to make sure that it's not too hard. The petal-like formation at the base of the fruit tells you how many segments there are inside. The taste, aroma and texture of mangosteens are quite unique. They are known as the queen of tropical fruit. Thais believe them to be a 'cool' or 'yin' fruit which can balance the effect of 'hot' or 'yang' fruit such as durian. They can help to cure stomach problems. In Thailand, the mangosteen season is from May to September. The skin can be used as a cloth dye.

Melon (Tang Thai)

A favourite Thai dessert is melon with coconut milk, but it all depends on choosing the right melon. For sweet tasting and fragrant melons, choose those with a tight, green-yellow skin. The patterns on the skin should be quite far apart from each other. If the skin looks slightly cracked, it means that the melon has fully ripened, so they're okay. These normally have yellow-ish-green meat. Thai restaurants usually serve melons with coconut milk, because they are sweet, similar to cantaloupes. Other fruit eaten with melons include sweet corn, black sticky rice, taro, or mangluck. Once you've tasted melon with coconut milk, you're bound to fall in love with other fruit eaten in this uniquely Thai way.

Papaya (Ma-la-kor)

Papaya trees are quite easy to grow, and the fruit has many uses. Unripe papaya is very high in vitamin C, and the enzyme papain found in papaya tree sap is used to marinate meat. Add a few drops to the boiling water to soften meat. Ripe papayas turn yellow-orange on the inside and a brilliant orange-red inside. Papayas grow all year round in Thailand and are high in vitamins A and C. Unripe ones help with the process of digestion and also cure indigestion. Ripe ones are a mild tonic.

Pineapple (Sup-pa-rod)

Pineapples can be sweet-and-sour or just plain sweet. A favourite in Thailand is the Phuket pineapple which is smaller and crisper, with a deep yellow colour and unique aroma. With the help of a blender, a pineapple makes a refreshing drink either by itself or mixed with assorted fruits. It also makes a delicious sorbet. Thai seaside restaurants like to serve rice or fried rice in a hollowed-out pineapple, especially Khao Ob Sup-pa-rod (Baked Fried Rice in Pineapple). It's a perfect container, and some of the taste and aroma is infused in the rice. Pineapple juice also has medical uses. It can relieve sores, cuts, and swelling. Eaten regularly, pineapple helps to prevent gum problems. Thais are lucky to have pineapples all year round.

Pomegranate (Thab-thim)

The Chinese in Thailand believe pomegranates bring good luck. They are always seen in wedding feasts and at other festivals and ceremonies. The smooth glossy skin is dark green when young, but turns greenish-orange or red when they ripen. Inside the segmented flesh is a deep red, which gives them their Thai name, thab-thim, or ruby. When eaten, the segments burst into liquid with a sweet and sour taste. They are highly nutritious and good for stomach problems. The skin and roots can be used to make an antiseptic. The only reason they are not more popular is that they are rather expensive.

Pomelo (Som-O)

The pomelo is one of the many kinds of citrus fruit found in Thailand. They are round and big, with thick green skin. The colour of the fruit ranges from whitish yellow to whitish pink to fresh pink. They can be very sweet, or slightly sour. The ones grown in Thailand are kao nam pueng, tong dee, kao pan and kao puang. These are mainly found in Nakorn Pathom. Pomelos can be eaten fresh by just peeling off the skin and the thin white protective layers. Medicinally, pomelos help to clear the throat and to relieve a cough. They are good for the stomach since they help with digestion and cure asthma.

Rambutan (Ngoh)

Rambutans belong to the same family as lychees and longans. They are egg-shaped with a bright red/yellow skin and long, soft spines. Inside, the translucent white flesh is wrapped round an almond-shaped seed. The flesh should be sweet with just a hint of sourness. Thailand has two types. Ngoh rong rien have a bright red skin with green tips on the spines. They are grown in abundance in the south. Ngoh chompu have a pink skin with longer spines. They are grown in the east. Both types normally bear fruit between May and September.They are rich in vitamin C, calcium and phosphorous when fresh and can provide relief for chronic diarrhoea.

Roseapple (Chom-phoo)

Some types are bell-shaped, some look like a fluted pyramid. All have a glossy smooth, thick and juicy skin, which can be light green, light pink or bright red. Inside is mostly hollow with some spongy pith. The whole fruit can be eaten except the pip. The taste is delicate but very refreshing. Of the many varieties, the chompu mam has a pink skin and a sweeter taste, while chompu muang petch are translucent green with a very tempting aroma, and chompu tien is pink and less tasty but is usually eaten with a dip of dried powdered chilli mixed with salt. They are available in Thailand all year round, but are most abundant from October to March.

Salak (Ra-kam)

Salak are also called 'snake fruit', because of their shape. Their brown skin is covered with thorns, but this doesn't mean that they are difficult to peel. Just peel them very carefully. The fruit is brown, normally with three segments attached tightly together. It is quite sour, though sometimes sweet. You can eat them in syrup and ice, but make sure you take out the stone first.

Santol (Ga-ton)

These are round, slightly flat with yellow skin and beige fruit. The seeds are white and fluffy like cotton. They contain three distinctive tastes: sour and rubbery, sweet and sour and completely sweet. There are two varieties in Thailand. The first are local santols, or jungle santols, which are small and flat and sweet. Sometimes they have a hint of sour. Hor santols, or sweet santols, are larger and sweeter. They're eaten fresh with salt mixed with chilli powder. Before eating, they're normally cracked on the floor since this improves the taste. Peeled pieces of santols are also eaten with syrup and ice. They can be kept longer by preserving them in saltwater.

Sapodilla (La-mud)

Sapodillas are sweet and have a pleasant taste. In Thailand, they're available from October to December. You should choose long, slender ones, with light brown, tight skin. The meat should be aromatic, soft, and brownish red in colour. They have a black stoneso be careful when giving them to children. They are normally eaten when fully ripened, since if they are unripe, they will have a very rubbery, unpleasant taste. Once cleaned, the skin may also be eaten, but they are better when peeled.

Star fruit (Ma-fueng)

Star fruit are long with a cross-section like a six-pointed star. Unripe ones are clear green while ripe ones are yellow. The taste varies a lot. Some are quite sour, some are sour-sweet, and some are completely sweet. Thais like to eat them a little under-ripe when they are crisp and slightly sour. Dipping them in powdered chilli and salt makes them taste much juicier. Over-ripe ones are no good. Star fruit can be preserved either dried or pickled. The season runs from October to December. Apart from its beautiful shape, star fruit also has medicinal qualities such as curing gallstone or acting as a diuretic. Some believe they can cure hangovers.

Water Chestnut (Haew)

Two ways of eating Thai desserts are with coconut milk and with syrup. Melons are eaten with coconut milk, but water chestnuts are better with syrup. Simply boil the chestnuts and peel off the black skin which will bring you to the transparent, yellow, rich and creamy meat. If they are too expensive, buy them in a can from supermarkets. Whichever way they come, just add syrup and ice to them and you have yourself a dessert. You can also eat them with sweet corn or jackfruit. The Thais say that if a boy's love is not reciprocated, he is like a water chestnut.

Watermelon (Tang Mo)

Technically, watermelons are a vegetable but they are eaten as a fruit. The two types found in Thailand are Sugarbaby which has a dark green skin, and the Charlton Grey which is light green with round dots. The inside can be yellow or red. Both taste the same but the yellow ones cost more. The Chinese use them in special ceremonies because the colour yellow represents gold—the symbol of wealth. They are available nearly all year round. The dried pips make a popular snack called med kuay jee. Watermelons are extra juicy and ideal for making sweet fruit juice, Phon-la-mai Pun (Assorted Fruit Squash), to quench your thirst or to cure fevers.

Acacia (Cha-om)

Cha-om is a medium-sized, thorny bush with a slightly unpleasant smell. Thais like to pick the shoots, deep-fry them dipped in egg, and eat them with rice and chilli paste. It's a simple dish but one that many people love. This is another vegetable full of nutrition. It can help reduce the risk of cancer and heart disease.

Angled gourd (Buab Liam)

Angled gourds are long and oval with ten ridges. Choose the small ones with a fresh green colour and sharp ridges. These will be sweeter and tastier. The whole vegetable can be eaten, including the skin which is rich in nutrition. Only the sharp ridges need to be pared away.

Thais love to use boiled angled gourd to dip in chilli paste. Or to add to Gaeng Liang (Spicy Mixed Vegetable Soup). Or to boil in clear soup. A slightly different kind called the sponge gourd has a finer texture. The dried gourd can be used as a sponge-like scourer much like a loofa.

Asparagus (Nor Mai Farang)

The Thai name for asparagus translates as "western bamboo". It is not related to bamboo, but Thais think it looks like a bamboo shoot and eat it in the same way. Compared to western asparagus, the Thai version is crisper and has a greener taste. Thais love to stir-fry asparagus in oyster sauce, or include it in Phad Phak Ruam Mit (Sauteed Mixed Vegetables), a favourite of all vegetarians.

Apart from its enticing taste, asparagus is a source of glutathione which helps prevent cancer. It also contributes to the sperm-alert diet. Asparagus spears are not hard to store. Keep them in water, just as you would flowers, and cover with cling-film.

Aubergine (Ma-khue Chang)

Aubergines are an Asian vegetable that has become very popular in the United States. Large aubergines have waxy purple skin with green stalks. They can be used to make many dishes depending on what the chef wants. You can slice them into thin pieces and wrap them in seasoned minced pork in the same way you'd wrap fried wontons. Steam them and you will have yourself a delicious appetizer. If you want to try to improve the taste, put some gaeng kiew warn with chicken on it before serving. If you like eggs, dip them in eggs before frying.

Baby-corn

Baby-corn (Khao Phod Orn)

Baby corn are corn ears which have not germinated and grown to full size. They are eight to ten centimetres long. The outer fibre casing is discarded, and the rest can be eaten whole. They are sweet and crispy and make a great nibble.When buying, pick out those with a fresh-looking colour and no trace of insects. They are not difficult to grow in the garden too. All you need to do is keep an eye out for male shoots and pinch them out, so that the females don't get a chance to germinate.

Bamboo Shoot

Bamboo Shoot (Nor Mai)

Bamboo shoots have a lot of food value. Fresh shoots contain amino acids essential to the body system, and also fiber which reduces the risk of cancer in the intestine. Shoots grown in cooler regions in the hills are the sweetest. They should be boiled for twenty to thirty minutes to soften the texture and bring out the taste. Bamboo shoots can also be stored for the off-season. Thai housewives slice them into strips and bottle them in brine. Nowadays you can buy them the same way in cans.

Banana Buds

Banana Bud (Hua Plee)

The banana tree is truly a marvel. Besides the fruit, the leaves and trunk also have their uses. The shoots make an unusual and nutritious form of vegetable. The banana shoots appear at the top of the tree alongside the bunches of ripening fruit. They are curved and reddish-pink and can be picked when about a foot long. They are used as an accompaniment for chilli paste dip, as an ingredient of various curries, and as a garnish for Phad Thai Goong Sod (Fried Rice Noodles with Prawns). Their crispy texture and unusual light taste makes a delicious Yam Hua Plee (Spicy Banana Shoot Salad).

Beansprouts (Thua Ngok)

Bean sprouts are easy to grow. Just soak beans in water and keep in a damp place for three to four days. You can use many types of beans, but soybeans give a fatter, juicier sprout. They can be stored for a long time by in water or in the fridge. Leave the root strand on, because if this is removed they rot quicker. You can cook them with the root. Bean sprouts are usually stir-fried with tofu or eaten in soup. The Chinese like to add raw, crispy bean sprouts to bowls of noodles.

Bell Pepper (Phrik Yuak)

These are also known as capsicum or sweet chillies and come from the same family as chillies. They are popular in Chinese cooking and are quite spicy and aromatic. Thailand's bell peppers are smaller than those from Europe. The Chinese prepare the chillies by stir-frying them with meat or other vegetables. The secret is in the amount of time spent stir-frying them. Chinese chefs will not spend too long on them, otherwise they will lose their crispiness. Dishes which are great with bell pepper include chicken with cashew nuts, and fish in sweet and sour sauce.

Bottle gourd (Nam Tao)

A young bottle gourd has a delicate taste, somewhere between a cucumber and a gourd. When ripe, the skin becomes so thick they are no good for eating but have other uses. Traditionally the skin was used as a water-bottle, plate or bowl, and even made into masks and musical instruments like drums. In emergency, the gourd skin can be used as a flower vase. Nutritionally they are not of great value, but they taste good and go well with other vegetables. They are commonly found in Gaeng Liang (Spicy Mixed Vegetable Soup) and other vegetable dishes. Take care because over-cooking reduces them to a mush.

Cabbage (Ga-lam Plee)

Cabbages originally came from Europe but now are grown all over Thailand, especially in the hills. There are various kinds. Green, white or purple. Dense or loose. Round or heart-shaped. Apart from their ability to soothe a burning tongue, they are very high in vitamin C. They also contain elements which help reduce the risk of cancer and in some countries, fresh cabbages are eaten to ease pancreas problems. Wash with salt water or vegetables to flush out traces of agricultural chemicals. Fresh cabbages can be stored for a long time, but they may also be preserved, salted or dried.

Carrot (Kae-rot)

Carrots are native to Asia but have never played a large part in Thai cuisine. Even their Thai name is just a transliteration. Nowadays they appear often in salads and as garnish. And they are used for some sweets. But there are no major carrot dishes from the Thai kitchen.

Cassava (Man Sam-pa-lang)

Though cassava is not originally from Thailand, it grows very well there because it needs arid, dry land. Their leaves are green with five partings, similar to a hand, and they contain amino acids and various other proteins. They can be transported quite easily . However, one negative factor about them is the tree itself. It can kill humans and animals if eaten since it contains poisonous cyanide. Before cooking, ensure that the cassava is boiled and washed out first to eliminate any cyanide. Their young shoots are good when boiled and eaten with chilli paste dip.

Cauliflower (Dok Ga-lam)

The cauliflower is not a traditional Thai vegetable, but they are now grown widely in the hilly parts and on sale everywhere. Cauliflowers are known for their quantity of vitamin C which helps prevent cancer, and reduces risks of heart disease. One cauliflower provides the daily bodily requirement of vitamin C. If the vegetables are boiled or chopped and left out of the fridge, though, all their essential qualities will disappear. To store, one should wrap the entire vegetable in clingfilm or put it in a plastic container and store in the refrigerator.

Chinese Bitter Gourd (Ma-ra)

Ma-ra is also known as balsam pear, bitter cucumber or bitter melon. The bitter, almost medicinal taste is quite a surprise. But this bitterness also contains vitamins A and C which makes this a valuable vegetable. Thais believe the Ma-ra helps build up a good appetite and relieves mild indigestion. The bitterness can be reduced by soaking first in salt water, poaching, or boiling for a long time. Housewives pick out the younger ones, with light green colour and smooth skin, as these are tastier and have higher vitamin content than the fully ripe ones.

Chinese Cabbage (Phak Kwang Toong)

The Chinese cabbage is native to Asia. The leaves are dark green and the flowers are yellow. There are many kinds. Some grow as high as a foot. Others are short and fat, and are known as hongtay (emperor) cabbages. Another kind which originates from the west of China has black seeds which are pressed to make a pungent oil like mustard oil. This is great as a dip for fresh spring onions. Vitamin C is more concentrated in cabbage than in any other vegetable. We recommend eating it fresh because that way it retains most of its vitamins. Cabbage is also considered to be good for the eyes and good for the weight-conscious because of its minimal fat content.

Chinese Celery (Khuen-chai)

Khuen-chai is found in Asia and Europe, though the Asian variety is smaller and more delicate. The leaves are similar to coriander, but larger and with a stronger smell. When eaten fresh, it is rich in vitamin C. Thais believe it helps strengthen the immune system. It is often included in fish dishes because it reduces the fishy smell. The leaves can also be used to make a health drink. Chinese celery is very rich in vitamins and low in sodium so it is good for those with bladder problems. It also has beta-carotene which is good for the heart, helps prevent cancer and enlarges the blood vessels thus lowering blood pressure. It is very low in calories.

Chinese chives (Gui-chai)

Chinese chives add both flavour and aroma. They look like a fleshy grass topped by a small yellow flower. They can be stir-fried with crispy pork or fried with squid in Phad Gui-chai Pla Muek (Fried Squid with Chinese Chives). They contain essential elements such as calcium, phosphorous, iron, vitamin B and vitamin C. The green type contains more calcium and phosphorous than the white.

Coconut Shoots (Yod Ma-phrao Orn)

Yod ma-phrao orn is the tip of a young new leaf of the coconut tree. Special trees are grown and cut down to harvest these shoots. They have a firm but soft texture, a slightly sweet taste, and no smell. They are a good ingredient in soups, especially Gaeng Lueng (Spicy Coconut Shoot Soup), or they are stir-fried with chilli and fish or vegetables. They contain essential food elements such as calcium and phosphorous.

Coriander (Phak Chee)

Coriander leaves are used to decorate many dishes, and the whole plant is also used in cooking. The stem is pounded with garlic and black pepper for seasoning meat and for reducing the smell of fish. The leaf is often added to Tom Yam and other soups. To keep coriander fresh, put it in a glass with water just covering the roots, cover with clingfilm, and place in the refrigerator. Make sure you refill the water every couple of days and it will stay fresh for a week.

Cowslip Creepers (Dok Kha-jon)

Cowslip creepers are small light green flowers with a fragrant smell. The pretty flowers are often used in traditional decorations like the banana leaf container (gra-thong bai tong). The fruit are like cotton bolls, only smaller and flatter. When ripe, they burst open to release the seed. The shoots, flowers and fruit can all be cooked in many ways: Blanched and eaten with chilli paste dip. Stir-fried as a vegetable. Stuffed in an omelette. Or added as an ingredient in clear soup and Gaeng Som (Spicy and Sour Green Papaya Soup). They are high in vitamins A, B and C as well as other elements. Their roots also have medicinal qualities and are used for making eye-drops, for curing dizziness and for rousing the taste buds.

Crisp Eggplant (Ma-khue Proh)

There are lots of different eggplants in Thai cooking including mini eggplant, crisp eggplants, long eggplants, yellow eggplants and purple eggplants. The ones used in dishes such as Gaeng Khiew Wan Gai (Green Chicken Curry) are crisp eggplants because they blend in perfectly with the coconut milk. For those who prefer something crispier, they should use mini pea-sized eggplants instead. These vegetables contain calcium and iron which are good for the blood. Some believe they are an aid to digestion and blood circulation too. Choose those with a fresh green colour and don't store them too long as they will become bitter.

Cucumber (Tang Gwa)

Cucumbers have little food value. They are mostly water, which means they store easily and form a good contrast to spicy foods. Hence they are often used as a side decoration for many dishes, and also go well with chilli dip. Cucumbers are also prepared in a sauce called Ar-jad (Cucumber Sauce) which is eaten with Satay. Their high water content also helps to relieve fever, thirst and burns, and to flush out the body. Thin slices of cucumber placed on the face helps to hydrate and revitalize the skin. Their leaves are also a good for relieving stomach upsets. Cucurbitacin C found in the leaves, stalks and flesh helps prevent cancer.

Dried Beans (Thua Hang)

Thai cooking has lots of beans. For vegetarians they are an essential source of protein and food elements which others find in meat. Soya beans have the highest protein content. In non-vegetarian food, the main use of beans is in desserts. Beans of all sorts including soya beans, the bigger red kidney beans, the small (mung) green beans, and many others are boiled in sugar syrup and eaten with crushed ice. A favourite version is Thua Khiew Tom (Sweet Boiled Mung Bean).

Dried Chillies (Phrik Hang)

Thais love the aroma of roasted dried chilli and often sprinkle them into Thai salad dishes and Tom Yam. The chillies chosen for drying are usually the larger kind, two to three inches long. They are picked red and ripe and dried in the sun for two or three days.For using dry, first roast them lightly in a dry pan to bring out the flavour. This process can give off a sharp smell which irritates nose and eyes. To prevent this, sprinkle some salt in the pan before adding the chillies. After roasting, you can either use them whole, chop them up, or pulverize them with a mortar and pestle or electric blender to make your own chilli powder.

Dried Mushrooms (Hed Hom Hang)

Dried mushrooms offer a convenient and tasty source of protein. The most popular type in Thailand are Hed Hom because Thais believe that they help build up the immune system, reduce fat in blood vessels and prevent the formation of gallstones. Hed Hom are round and light to dark brown in colour with white gill-like slits. They are grown widely in Japan and China and in the hills of northern Thailand where the temperature is lower. Before using the dried mushrooms, soak them in water until they soften a bit.

Eggplant (Ma-khue Yao)

Ma-khue yao is the large, long form of eggplant. It comes in many colours—white, yellow, light green, purple, and purply-black. But all have the same smooth texture inside. Thais eat them both fresh and cooked. Young ones have a lighter, sweeter taste, and are good eaten raw alongside chilli paste, or fried in eggs. The riper ones have a little more taste and bitterness. Both young and ripe are used in curry soups such as Gaeng Khiew Wan Gai (Green Chicken Curry). For making a Tam Ma-khue Yao (Spicy Eggplant Salad), the eggplants are first grilled gently and then mixed with other ingredients. This is a popular snack with drinkers.

Fresh Chillies (Phrik Sod)

Today Thai food is closely associated with chilli. The plant was introduced by the Portuguese in the sixteenth century. Chillies come in different types and sizes. Phrik Khee Noo is the smallest kind, about a centimetre long, but also the hottest. Phrik Chee Fah is three to four inches long and can be red, green and yellow. If you cannot take the hotness, just split the chilli open and throw away the seeds. That is the hot part. Spicy food can affect the digestive system by preventing food being absorbed properly. But eaten moderately, chilli stimulates blood circulation and can help prevent heart disease or cancer.

Galangal (Kha)

Galangal

Galangal is a root like ginger but larger with a milky-white flesh and pink-tinged skin. It gives a distinctive, lightly acid taste and helps reduce the smell of meat. Galangal contains oils such as eugenal, cineol and camphor. These oils help to stimulate digestion and reduce flatulence. Galangal is also taken to soothe infested tonsils, and to clear the throat of phlegm. Some people crush the bulb and boil it in water as a preparation to cure indigestion or stomach upsets. Galangal is easy to grow in the garden, and has the added benefit of a beautiful bright red flower.

Galingale (Gra-chai)

Galingale

Galingale functions as both herb and vegetable. It's easy to grow in the back garden. Just plant the bulb in sandy soil and keep watering it. The bulb develops shoots and must be harvested before it flowers. Both the yellow root and the shoots can be eaten. Galingale is used to make curries, especially with fish, and can be used as a substitute for garlic in many dishes. Boil the root for a drink which reduces flatulence.

Garlic (Gra-thiam)

Garlic

Thai garlic has smaller cloves than the western kind, and the smell is stronger. It is one of the basic ingredients of many types of Thai food. Just about the only dish that doesn't use garlic is dessert! Garlic is medically proven to contain allicin which can reduce the level of cholestorol in the blood. Some believe that eating ten to fifteen cloves of garlic a day reduces the risk of heart disease. If fresh garlic is kept for too long, it loses this benefit, but gra-thiam dong or pickled garlic retains the property. Because of this, it is often quite expensive.

Ginger (Khing)

Ginger adds flavour to Thai cooking and also serves as a medicinal preparation. The root is boiled to make nam khing (ginger juice) which is taken in cases of a light fever, runny nose or indigestion. Some people drink it regularly as a tonic.In Thai cooking, ginger is used for all kinds of dishes including desserts. The root can be chopped julienne-style and added to Thai salads or used as a side accompaniment to appetizers like northern Thai sausage. Ginger grows very easily. Just buy a fresh root and plant it in the garden. Their yellowish green flowers will brighten up your day.

Gourd (Fak)

The Thai gourd has a green skin with a waxy gloss, and hence is sometimes called a wax gourd. There are both round and long varieties. The flesh is soft and juicy though rather bland. It is a popular ingredient of the side soups which act as a blander counterpoint to the other spicy dishes in a Thai meal.

According to both Chinese and Thai medicinal lore, gourds have the ability to flush poisons out of the body, and can serve as a diuretic to relieve fevers.

Grathin(Gra-thin)

The gra-thin is a variety of acacia or wattle, often found in household hedges. Traditionally these trees were used to mark boundaries. And because they have so many uses, Thai households like to have one close at hand. The little leaves are delicate and slightly scented. They can be chewed or added to salads, and are beneficial for the nervous system. The shoots, flowers and young pods are often eaten with chilli paste dip. The flowers are good for the liver. Even the root is believed to relieve flatulence and prolong life.

Kaffir Lime (Ma-grood)

Apart from being a kind of seasoning, kaffir limes are also used as herbs. They are small, thorny plants. They are light to dark green in colour. They have a pleasant smell because the Citronella stores evaporating oil. The limes come in various shapes. Some are smooth skinned and some have uneven skin. The juice is very sour and its smell helps to get rid of the stench of fish. The juice contains citric acid which gets rid of soap stains. They also help to cure indigestion as it increases the appetite. The oil from the skin can help darken hair and make it look glossy.

Kaffir Lime leaves (Bai Ma-grood)

These are fleshy and glossy leaves with a strong limy aroma which contributes astringency to many dishes including Tom Yam (Spicy Soup). They also contain the cancer preventative, beta-carotene. Young kaffir lime leaves in coconut milk is an unusual and rather rare dish which makes a great accompaniment to a chilli paste dip.

Kale (Ka-nah)

Kale is a vegetable that originally came from China and later became very popular in southeast Asia. There are two types distinguished by the shape of the leaf. The type with shorter, fleshier leaves is more delicious than the long thin leaves. The dark green kale leaves contain many essential vitamins, including vitamin C that helps build up the immune system and beta-carotene that helps prevent cancer. Both the stalks and leaves are edible, but the stalks are probably crunchier and tastier.

Khilek (Khi-lek)

Khilek is a medium-sized bush of the cassia family. The little leaves taste so bitter it is amazing that anyone ever bothered to try cooking them. But once cooked and tasted, they become irresistible. Gaeng khi-lek is a local Thai favourite. The leaves, flowers and young shoots are all edible. They should be boiled two to three times over and left for a while to get rid of their notorious bitterness. You can mix up some curry paste, dried chilli, galingale, galangal, garlic, onion, shrimp paste, and pre-cooked snakehead fish (a freshwater fish), add some coconut milk, season with fish sauce, and stir until boiling. Then, add some of the pre-boiled khi-lek. It's still bitter, but for many people it's delicious.

Lemongrass (Ta-krai)

The plant looks like a clump of rough grass with a lemony aroma, and hence the English name of "lemongrass". The thick, woody base of each leaf has long been a key ingredient in Thai cooking. It mixes well with lemon as part of the distinctive taste of Tom Yam Goong (Spicy Prawn Soup). It helps smother the strong smell of meat. It is chopped and sprinkled in Thai salads to infuse them with a sour taste and fresh aroma. For this purpose, the outer layers of the leaf stem must be peeled away until you reach a pinkish layer.

The oil responsible for the plant's aroma is a good cure for upset stomach and indigestion. Lemongrass juice is a popular herbal drink in Thai traditional medicine.

Lettuce (Phak Gad Hom)

Thai lettuce has a dark green leaf with a crinkly edge. It is used both as a vegetable and as a decoration for many dishes. It appears in salads, but is also used as a wrapping for dishes like Larb E-sarn (Spicy Northeastern-style Minced Pork Salad). Spoon the dish into a leaf, wrap it up, and pop it into your mouth.

Like other green vegetables, the lettuce is high in vitamin C and can also help reduce the risk of cancer. But lettuce should never be cooked as its store of vitamin C quickly disappears, and its shapely leaf collapses.

Long Beans (Thua Fak Yao)

They are sometimes known as cow peas or yard beans because they can grow over thirty centimetres in length. Long beans are crunchy and tasty. They have a high concentration of vitamin C which promotes absorption of the iron needed to keep blood in a healthy state. They also help reduce cholesterol. Choose the beans that look firm, bright green, and not crooked. Always clean them properly to get rid of traces of chemicals. This should be done either by running them under the tap or leaving them in salt water or in vinegar for about 10 minutes.

Lime (Ma-now)

Limes are very versatile. They add a dash of sourness to tea, to fresh fruit, or to seafood. A slice of lime gives a touch of colour to a seafood plate or a refreshing drink. Squeezed limes make a great thirst-quencher which also helps to revitalize and relieve weariness. The lime tree is small and thorny with small white flowers. The fruits are round, yellow-green, and packed with vitamin C. Oil extracted from the skin or leaves can be used to treat diarrhoea, flatulence and gum disease, as well as relieving a cough or blocked nose. The sourness of lime comes from the various acids which help digest food such as citric acid, molic acid or quinic acid.

Mini Chinese Bitter Gourd (Ma-ra Khee-nok)

These are smaller in size and even more bitter in taste than the common ma-ra or bitter gourd. But for many Thais this makes them even better. They are rich in vitamin C and people in the olden days believed that they had many medicinal properties including the treatment of diabetes. They are still used to build appetite and to stimulate the liver. The leaves are boiled as a treatment for indigestion. The Chinese eat them to relieve acne on the face and body.

Thais love eating them with chilli paste dip, but not fresh because they are very bitter. They first have to be boiled with at least one change of water, or soaked for a time in a solution of water and salt.

Mint (Sa-ra-nae)

Thai mint has leaves which are round, serrated and slightly thicker than the common European variety. Their main use in Thai cooking is as a flavouring in salads such as Larb E-sarn (Spicy Northeastern-style Minced Pork Salad) and Yam Woon Sen (Spicy Vermicelli Salad). They are sometimes mixed together with other fresh ingredients to smother the smell of fish.

The menthol aroma is a pick-me-up. Mint is taken to relieve headache, and to reduce flatulence or perspiration. The leaves can also be crushed and rubbed on the skin to relieve insect bites.

Morning Glory (Phak Boong)

Phak boong or Phak tod yod is known as water convolvulus, water morning glory, water spinach, and swamp cabbage. There are several variants. The Chinese morning glory has the leaves that look young and juicy and avoid those with yellowing stalks because they will be too chewy. Thai field morning glory has narrow leaves with red tips. Thai water morning glory has fatter leaves with both red and green tips.Morning glory soothes ulcers and is good for diabetics who need to control their sugar intake. According to an old saying, eating morning glory makes for pretty eyes. Probably this comes from its vitamin A and iron.

Mushrooms (Hed)

Thailand has lots of mushrooms and fungi, some edible and some not. Angel mushrooms come from the same family as abelone mushrooms. They grow quickly and easily on rotten wood or any place that is moist, and so are not so expensive. They are thick, smooth and white and have a creamy, slightly sweet taste which works well in many dishes .Mouse-ear mushrooms come in two kinds—white and black. The white ones look like human ears or flower petals. They are soft and have a light taste. The black ones are jelly-like, light brownish black in colour and grow on wood. They are sweet, tender, chewy and popular in Thai dishes too.

Onion (Hom Yai)

Thai onions are sweeter than European ones, and generally lack any trace of sourness. If eaten fresh, they are crunchy and slightly hot, which makes them an important ingredient in Thai salads. When cooked they become sweeter, and are popular as a filling for omelettes, and as an ingredient in fried rice. The rings can also be deep-fried in batter and eaten as a snack or side dish. The aromatic juice of onions is extracted for use in drinks and sweets such as jelly.

Onions contain elements which reduce the risk of heart disease and blood disorders.

Pandan (Bai Toey)

Pandan is a bush with long, narrow green leaves with a distinctive scent. The leaves are used for adding colour and aroma to dishes and desserts. Chicken wrapped in the leaf has the distinctive look and taste of Gai Hor Bai Toey (Deep-fried Chicken in Pandan Leaves). Sweets such as Woon Ga-thi (Pandan Jelly with Coconut Cream) get their attractive green colour from the leaf. Boiled with soya beans, the leaves make a compress used to treat athlete's foot. The flowers can also be boiled to make a juice which helps relieve a cold. The leaves are often found as part of the offerings Thais make to images of the Buddha.

Peppercorns (Phrik Thai)

The lovely smell of pepper makes any dish irresistible. The pepper plant is a vine. The young peppercorns start off green, and gradually change to yellow, bright orange, and then red when they are fully ripe. The fresh peppercorns are added to dishes like spicy stir-fried catfish or wild boar. When dried, the peppercorns turn black. To make white pepper, the red ripe peppercorns are peeled and soaked in water before drying. Apart from the colour, white and black pepper also taste differently. Black pepper is stronger in both taste and smell whereas white pepper can irritate the nose. Thais use the powdered black pepper.

Pickled Cabbage

Pickled Cabbage (Phak Gad Dong)

Pickled cabbage is popular with rice porridge, as an ingredient in yam (Thai salads) or gaeng jeud (clear soups), or simply as an appetizer or garnish. Pickling is easy. Wash the leaves thoroughly, put them in a bowl of salt water, and leave the bowl uncovered for three to four days. To make it tastier, put some alum in the water. Pickled cabbage can also be bought ready-made in cans and jars.

Pumpkin

Pumpkin (Fak Thong)

Also known as winter squash, they come from Central America but are now well loved across Asia. They have brown skin and golden yellow flesh. When choosing, always go for the small ones. If you like them strong in flavour and firm, you should keep them to ripen for a few days. The combination of richness and sweetness in pumpkins make them perfect in dishes .The yellowness of pumpkins contains beta-carotene which helps prevent cancer. They also contain elements which help control the blood sugar level, prevent diabetes, nourish the liver, and help eyesight.

Radish

Radish (Hua Phak Gad)

The Thai radish is a root vegetable like a big white carrot. They have a slightly sweet taste with a trace of hotness. They should be bought and eaten fresh because they quickly shrivel and lose their sweetness. Their main appearance in Thai cooking is sliced and added to beef stock soup. They are also one of the ingredients used in Thai Sukiyaki.

Radishes can also be eaten fresh like the French and Germans do, or included as an ingredient in salads. The vitamin C in a radish helps prevent cancer and helps to build up the immune system. When preserved, they have a sweet and salty taste and are called Hua chai po.

Red Basil (Ga-phrao)

Ga-phrao has a sweet, pungent, herby aroma. It is one of the most common and most distinctive ingredients in Thai food. There are two kinds - white basil and red basil. They are often used along with chilli in meat dishes where they help reduce the meaty smell. Basil can help combat indigestion. It contains beta-carotene which prevents cancer and blood disorders, and also phosphorous and calcium which strengthen the bones. When the leaves have all been used, try sticking the stems in moist soil. The leaves will grow back in a few days.

Roselle (Gra-jiab)

The roselle tree has many little-known uses. The small fruits can be either red or green with a sharp tip. They help clear the throat, cure indigestion, regulate blood pressure, cleanse the intestines, kill germs, develop brain cells and relieve stomach problems. They can be boiled to make a juice which is good for cleaning wounds. Dried roselle can be used to make a sour-tasting tea which acts as a diuretic, helps cure gallstone, relieves cough and fever, and revitalizes the body and mind. For storing, first soak the fruit in lime juice overnight then leave in water for another night and in syrup for another night. Dry under the sun and leave in syrup for another four days until they turn crystal-like.

Sawtooth Coriander (Phak Chee Farang)

In Thai, sawtooth coriander is called 'farang' (foreign) coriander. The taste is rather bland, and its popularity in Thai cooking is mostly because it retains its attractive green colour even after cooking. For this reason it is added to dishes which would otherwise look duller and less enticing, such as Tom Yam (spicy soups), Larb E-sarn (Spicy Northeastern-style Minced Pork Salad), and Moo Yang Nam Tok (Spicy Marinated Pork Salad). It is also commonly used as a decoration. Fresh sawtooth coriander is high in vitamin C and contains elements which the body needs to build the vitamin A required for good eyesight and an overall healthy body.

Shallot (Hom Dang)

Thai red onions are sweet and aromatic. They are an essential ingredient in yam (Thai salad) and E-sarn larb because they contribute to the taste, aroma and appearance of the dish. Choose the larger, firm-looking onions with no wrinkles or blemishes on the outer skin. Peeling releases oils which can irritate the eyes, but you can prevent this by plunging the onions first into boiling water and then into cold water. Fried red onions are sprinkled on Khai Look-khoey (Fried Eggs with Tamarind Sauce) and other dishes. They are made the same way as fried garlic. Peel and chop finely, pre-heat the oil, add the onions and keep stirring over a low heat until they turn yellow and give off an aromatic smell.

Snow Peas (Thua Lan-tao)

These are the tender peas which can be eaten whole. In Thailand they tend to be smaller and tenderer than the western version. They can be eaten raw in salads, or stir-fried with other vegetables in Phad Phak Ruam Mit (Sauteed Mixed Vegetables). Choose the smaller ones with a fresh-green colour, and a soft pod.

The green in the peas contains beta-carotene which helps prevent cancer and heart disease. Like all kinds of peas and beans, snow peas are high in protein and are a good choice for people who want to cut down their intake of meat. In adddition, they contain vitamins, sodium, and fiber which helps the digestive system.

Spring Onion (Ton Hom)

These come coupled with coriander in terms of importance in Thai cooking. Apart from the pleasant smell, spring onions also have medicinal benefits, which is one reason why Asians love to add them to their food. The onions you select should be large and green with yellow tips and white stalks. Thais usually use them to decorate dishes.

Sweet Basil (Ho-ra-pha)

The taste of the sweet basil is similar to red basil but slightly milder. The stems are red. Italians use dried basil leaves for preparing salad dressings, but in the Thai kitchen, basil is used to add aroma to dishes. The oil in the leaves can be extracted to make a drink which is taken to improve appetite and to treat an indigestion that results from eating too much meat. The oil helps to kill germs, induce sweating and clear phlegm. Some people chew the leaves as a breath freshener. The chlorophyll in the leaves contains beta-carotene which helps prevent cancer and heart conditions.

Sweet Potato (Man Thed)

There are many kinds of sweet potatoes, but the ones often seen in Thailand are the potatoes with red or brown skin. The red-skinned potatoes are red inside, while the brown-skinned potatoes are yellow or white. You should select fresh, clean ones. Because the potatoes can grow virtually anywhere, they're commonly found in Asian countries where the weather can be quite volatile. Diced sweet potatoes are also used in desserts, particularly with sweetened coconut milk, diced yam, slices of banana, and sago balls. Sweet potatoes are very rich in vitamin A.

Taro (Puek)

Taro is a purple-skinned root vegetable with a rich sweetish taste. It is used in making several Thai sweets. It is also made into chunks or chips eaten as snacks. Peeling is difficult because it can irritate the skin between the fingers. The trick is to grill or sun-dry the taro first before peeling.

Tomato (Ma-khue Thed)

Tomatoes belong to the same family as chilli. There are thousands of varieties, from very tiny ones to huge ones. Choose the type according to the way you plan to use them. In Thailand, the tomatoes popular for eating fresh are small, pinkish varieties such as Seeda, Floradale or Calypso. Seeda is also commonly used for making Tom Yam. For cooking, choose tomatoes which are fleshy and not too watery. Select the ones which have a glossy skin with an even colour.

Tomatoes are delicious because they contain the amino acid, glutamic, which is the ingredient found in monosodium glutamate. Apart from their refreshing and appealing appearance and healthy qualities, tomatoes intensify the flavours of many dishes.

Turmeric (Kha-min)

Turmeric is a root from the same family as ginger. It has a brown skin and yellow flesh, which is dried and pounded to make turmeric powder. Turmeric figures strongly in cooking from the southern region because it counteracts the strong smell created by other ingredients popular in southern cuisine. Turmeric helps cure gallstones. It is also used as a cloth dye and as a skin treatment for producing softer, lighter skin. Freshly picked turmeric roots must be washed, and then boiled for one to six hours until they soften and turn bright yellow. Then they are dried so that they look tight-skinned. In this form, they can be stored for a long time.

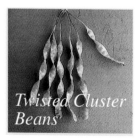

Twisted Cluster Beans (Sator)

Sator are giant beans which grow in a long, green and often twisted pod. Mostly they are grown in the south of Thailand. Each bean is two to four centemetres long. In the pod they rest in a layer of soft sticky fibre which has to be discarded. In fresh markets and supermarkets they can be bought already peeled in bags. Smell them for freshness before buying.

The beans are crisp and chewy with a slightly bitter taste and a strong smell. Some people love the smell, others hate it. Grilling the beans helps to reduce the smell. Sator are full of protein and energy too: twenty beans are the equivalent of two pieces of bread.

Water lily (Sai-bua)

Water lilies have not only flowers that please the eye, but also stems that fill the stomach. The hose-like stem can be eaten either fresh or cooked. They should first be washed, peeled and chopped into bite-size pieces before eating alongside favourites such as the chilli paste dip. They can also be fried. The flowers themselves can be stir-fried in vegetable oil, garlic, sugar and pepper. Both the stems and flowers can be added to a Gaeng Liang (Spicy Mixed Vegetable Soup).

Water Mimosa (Gra-ched)

This vegetable is also commonly known by Thais as 'puck roo non' (vegetables aware of bedtime) because when it gets dark, the leaves close up as if ready for bed. They grow in water. Both the stalks and leaves are eaten, but the white, woody part of the stem has first to be discarded. On first sight, gra-ched looks a little strange, but the taste is persuasive. They make a wonderful spicy Thai salad (yam), and are delicious in Gaeng Som. Most often, though, they are stir-fried using the same method as Phad Phak Boong (Sauteed Morning Glory with Fermented Whole Soybeans). Always choose fresh ones, wash thoroughly, and chop the vegetable at the last moment before cooking to retain the vitamins.

White Greens (Phak Gad Khao)

Sometimes called celery cabbages, there are two kinds. One has white stalks and yellowish-green leaves packed densely together. The other is more loosely formed, has darker green leaves, and is sometimes called green cabbage. They originate from northern China where they are often pickled in the form known best as Korean kimchi. Nowadays these cabbages are found everywhere in Asia, Europe and America.They are best picked and eaten while still slightly young, because then the leaves are crisp and the taste is greener than when they are fully ripe. Celery cabbage is a good basic vegetable which contains many essential food elements such as carbohydrates, fat, protein, sodium and vitamins.

Wild Pepper (Cha-phlu)

Cha-phlu is a local creeper with dark-green heart-shaped leaves with a slightly spicy flavour. In a favourite Thai dish, Miang Kum, you take a cha-phlu leaf, fold it into a cup shape, fill it with slivers of ginger, peanuts, dried shrimp, shallot and lime, and pop it into your mouth. The leaves are high in vitamins, sodium chloride and beta-carotene. But they also contain oxalate which can cause pancreas problems if you eat too much cha-phlu. Usually Thai dishes with cha-phlu also have meat since this neutralizes the bad effects of the oxalate. One such dish is roast chicken with wild pepper leaves.

Winged Beans (Thua Phu)

The winged bean is five to six inches long. In cross-section, the shape is square with wings on the corners. If eaten raw, they should be the young, flat pods that are fresh green in colour and have not yet developed beans. Choose the ones that are soft and have no black marks. They are high in protein and vitamin C and are good for the skin. According to old Thai medicinal lore, dried winged beans which have been roasted until yellow can be used to make a tea which is a good energy booster.

Yam Root (Man Gaew)

Yam root is a tuber out of which grows a creeping vine. The tuber is full of fluid and has a sweet but rather watery taste. It can be peeled and eaten fresh with a dip of salt and sugar to embellish the taste. Or mixed in a salad. The root can also be cooked in easy dishes such as stir-fried with minced pork, or made into a clear soup with pork rind.

The root is supposed to have many medicinal qualities such as relieving body heat, reducing fever and combatting a hangover. The seeds can be ground into a balm, but be careful because it is very poisonous if eaten. Villagers also grind the root to make a powder for killing animal ticks.

Chilli Sauce (Sauce Phrik)

If you eating Khai Yad Sai (Savoury Stuffed Omelettes) then a bowl of chill sauce on the side is de rigeur. For Thais, chilli sauce is used to lift the taste of all kinds of dishes. The most famous bottled brand is name Sriracha, and has a distinctive orange-red colour and sour-hot taste. It is not difficult to make your own. You will need 20 big red chillies (phrik chee fa), 10 small tomatoes, 20 cloves of garlic, 1/2 cup of vinegar, 1/2 cup of sugar and 2 tablespoons of salt. Wash and de-seed the chillies, peel and blanch the garlic, poach the tomatoes and peel off their skin. Mash everything together. Season with vinegar, sugar and salt and put in a blender. Transfer into a bottle and store in a fridge.

Chinese Plum Sauce (Nam Jim Buay)

This sweet-and-sour dip is popular with deep fried snacks and some kinds of seafood such as crab and crab sausage. A good substitute can be made with easily available ingredients. You will need a tablespoon of strawberry jam, a tablespoon of vinegar, 2 tablespoons of caster sugar, 1/4 teaspoon of salt and a tablespoon of water. Boil the ingredients together and reduce until you get the rich, sticky finish of Chinese plum sauce.

Chinese Spaghetti (Khanom Jeen)

Another type of noodles is Chinese spaghetti. These are made from glutinous flour. If you go to the market early in the morning, you will see people setting up these noodles on woven trays in small bundles. They can be made into various dishes like any other noodles such as Khanom Jeen Nam Ngeow (Chinese Spaghetti with Spare Ribs Soup), Khanom Jeen Sao Nam (Chinese Spaghetti with Coconut Sauce), Kanom Jeen Nam Phrik (Chinese Spaghetti with Sweet Chilli Paste), Khanom Jeen Nam Yaa (Chinese Spaghetti with Fish Curry Soup), and Khanom Jeen Phad (Fried Chinese Spaghetti).

Coconut Milk (Nam Ga-thi)

Coconut milk is the rich base for many Thai curries and sweet dishes. It is made by grating fresh ripe coconut, adding water, and squeezing through a sieve. The thickness depends on the volume of water added, and different dishes have different requirements. Fresh coconut milk can be stored for about 3 hours. If put in a sealed container like a jar or plastic bag, it goes off quickly. To store for a longer time, add a little salt, bring to a boil, and then keep in the fridge. Nowadays, ready-made coconut milk is available in cartons and cans.

Curry Paste (Phrik Gaeng)

Most Thai curries are based on a paste made from a mixture of fresh or dried chilli, coriander, lemongrass, garlic, onion and salt. The different pastes vary in taste and colour: red, green, orange and yellow. There are also special pastes for the southern favourite, Massaman Nuea (Massaman Beef Curry) , the northern specialty, Gaeng Hung Lay (Northern-style Pork Curry), and for a slightly different taste, Roasted Chilli Paste (Nam Phrik Phao). Nowadays, ready-made Thai curry pastes are available from oriental food stores.

Curry powder (Phong Ga-ree)

Curry powder is a blend of spices usually including turmeric and chilli. The idea originated from India. Muslims who migrated to Thailand brought along their curry powders and since then the blend has been adapted to Thai tastes and Thai ingredients. For example, Thai versions leave out the cinnamon and nutmeg found in many Indian mixes, but add more coriander and powdered curry leaves. Curry powder is used in dishes like Poo Phad Phong Ga-ree (Fried Yellow Curry Crab) and in many other soups and curries like Sa-tu Lin Wua (Ox-tongue Stew). It can also be sprinkled on your food to give it a last little lift.

Dark Soya Sauce (See-iew Dam)

Dark soya sauce is another basic seasoning for Thai cooking. It is thicker, sweeter, and may be slightly more expensive than white soya sauce. It can be used to season dishes such as Khai Phalo (Boiled Eggs with Five-Spice Soup), Guay Teow Lord(Flat Rice Noodles with Minced Pork), or Gaeng Hoh (Dried Northern-style Mixed Curry). No other sauces can replace dark soya sauce. This sauce can be found at the oriental market.

Dried Fish (Pla Hang)

Because Thailand has a large variety of food, especially fish, Thais really enjoy storing the fish using many different methods. For example, king mackerels are preserved by marinating them in salt. If using a large fish, cut it into small pieces. Dissolve a tablespoon of salt and leave the fish in it for about thirty minutes. When buying these fish, choose the ones which have a fresh colour and not too much crystallized salt forming on them. To prepare, wash the fish and steam for about 10 minutes. Let cool for a while and transfer to a container. Keep refrigerated. By doing this, the fish will stay fresh for months.

Dried Shrimps (Goong Hang)

Small shrimps are left to dry in the sun until they turn reddish orange. They have a concentrated salty and shrimpy taste which is an essential element in Som Tam (Papaya Salad) and Yam Woon Sen (Spicy Vermicelli Salad). They are also pounded up and added to dishes like Khanom Jeen Sao Nam (Chinese Spaghetti with Coconut Sauce). They are usually sold in plastic bags. It is a good idea to spread them out and air them to disperse the smell, then store them in a jar or plastic container in the refrigerator. It is also a good idea to grill or roast them lightly before use.

Eggs (Khai)

Chicken eggs and duck eggs have the same food value, but Thais feel duck eggs smell too strongly to be used as a fresh ingredient. To identify eggs that are really fresh, look at the shell. It should have tiny pores and not be too glossy. It's also best if they haven't been scrubbed clean. This removes the shell's fibrous outer layer which slows down evaporation and makes the egg store longer.

Fermented Whole Soybeans (Tao-jiaw)

Tao-jiaw adds protein and a distinctive salty flavour to many dishes. There are two types—dark and white. The dark fermented soybeans are soft with a pleasant smell. They are used in a popular savoury dip called Tao-jiaw Lon. To make, stir coconut milk over low heat, add fermented soybeans, pork, minced prawns, tamarind juice and fresh chillies, and blend evenly together. Dip fresh vegetables and enjoy. Fermented soybeans are also added to Phad Phak Boong (Sauteed Morning Glory with Fermented Whole Soybeans) and other vegetable dishes to enhance the nutrition and the flavour. They also appear as sauce for Khao Man Gai (Steamed Chicken Rice).

Fish Sauce (Nam Pla)

Fish sauce provides the salty dimension in Thai food. It is made from either freshwater or saltwater fish, but mostly saltwater fish because they are cheaper. It is high in protein as well as minerals and vitamins. You can buy a bottle from an oriental food store. Look for a very clear colour and no sediment (shake the bottle). Don't buy it if it has a metal cap which will rust. Nam Pla Phrik (Chillies in Fish Sauce) is the everyday condiment for adding saltiness and spiciness to prepared dishes.

Five-spice Powder (Krueng Phalo)

Five spice powder is an essential ingredient in the Chinese kitchen since it can add flavour and aroma to any dish. Five spice powder is used in Chinese ceremonies for paying respects to their ancestors but for the Thais, it is a seasoning for Khai Phalo (Boiled Eggs with Five Spice Soup). The powder is a mixture of anise, cinnamon, fennel, cloves and Syechun peppercorns. The Chinese use the powder as medicine to help cure indigestion, and get rid of phlegm. Be careful not to buy too much because it doesn't stay fresh for very long. You should store phalo in a glass jar in the fridge.

Oyster Sauce (Sauce Hoy Nang-rom)

Stir frying is the quickest method of cooking and is popular with the Chinese. Oyster sauce is an essential ingredient in most stir-fries. It is added to stir-fried vegetables and other fried dishes along with sweet basil. Each dish should be seasoned while stir-frying, because constant stirring helps the ingredients blend evenly. The sauce is also used to flavour dishes such as omelets before the eggs go in the pan. Oyster sauce is sold in bottles and can be found everywhere.

Rice (Khao)

Thais cannot imagine life without rice. The two main types are glutinous/sticky (khao neow) and non-glutinous (khao jao). Both grow the same way, but the grain of sticky rice is glossier and paler in colour.There are many varieties of non-sticky rice but the most famous is the jasmine or Thai fragrant rice. Less well-known but more nutritious is khao sorm mue, an unpolished form similar to brown rice. Because of the high vitamin content in the fiber, this type is growing in popularity.

Rice noodles (Sen Guay Teow)

In Thailand, noodles are most popular as a quick and varied lunch. Noodles originally came to Thailand with the Chinese. Now they are available in many varieties. The common white noodles are made from rice flour. Like pasta, they come in various shapes. Sen yai are big and flat. Sen mee are smaller and flat. Sen lek are small and round. Yellow noodles made from wheat flour, called ba-mee, are also good for noodle soup. For crispy noodles like Mee Grob Rad Nah (Crispy Rice Noodles with Gravy), first boil the noodles, then deep fry them in very hot oil until they turn a crispy golden brown.

Salt (Glua)

In Thailand both rock salt (sintao) and sea salt (samut) are used. Rock salt is dug out, mixed with water, and left to crystallize. However, sea salt is more popular. The long Thai coastline is lined with salt fields. Seawater is trapped in the field at high tide and then left to dry out under the sun. Near Bangkok there are large salt fields in Samut Songkhram and Petchburi which have become tourist attractions because of the picturesque windmills and blindingly white piles of salt. Sea salt is rich in iodine.

Thais use salt in cooking but rarely as a table condiment. To add saltiness, they prefer fish sauce. The exception is with fruit. Thais believe a dash of salt brings out the taste of fruits like papaya and pineapple.

Salted Soy Bean Paste (Nam Jim Yen Ta Fo)

The redness in Yen Ta Fo (Rice Noodles in Red Soup) comes from this paste. Without this paste, Yen Ta Fo would lose its distinctive quality and become plain pork noodles. The secret of yen ta fo seasoning is up to the chef, but the main ingredients include red tao jiaw which is a Chinese invention. Grind this together with vinegar and garlic, and add some salt and sugar to taste. Add fresh chillies if you like strong flavours. The taste of homemade yen ta fo sauce might vary, depending on the taste of each chef, whether they prefer spiciness or sourness. But whatever you do, don't forget red tao jiaw. Yen ta fo sauce can be found at any oriental market.

Sauce for Chicken (Nam Jim Gai)

Khao Neow Gai Yang (Marinated Grilled Chicken with Sticky Rice) is always irresistible, but it's not the same without the right sauce. This is not difficult to make. You will need 5 big red chillies (phrik chee fa) and 10 cloves of garlic. Crush the garlic. Add 1/2 teaspoon of salt, 2 tablespoons of vinegar, 2 tablespoons of sugar. Place over medium heat and bring to boil. Add a little water to cornflour to make a paste, and put this in the mix to thicken it. Leave to cool. Now add the crushed chillies, mix well together and you have a sauce which is sweet, sour, salty and hot all at the same time. Dip your chicken piece and take a bite. To save time, look for bottles of chicken sauce in your supermarket or oriental food store.

Shrimp Paste (Ga-pi)

Ga-pi is a dense paste made from ground shrimps. It has a purplish-black colour and a strong smell. Good ga-pi should be moist but not sloppy, and should have no sign of salt crystallizing. To store it, use a jar with a very tight seal. In cooking, garlic helps to soften ga-pi's rather strong smell.

Ga-pi is one of the oldest, commonest, and most distinctive ingredients of Southeast Asian cooking. In Thailand, it is the main ingredient of the many types of chilli paste dip which are eaten with fresh or cooked vegetables and small fried fish. Ga-pi is also used in some curries, especially Gaeng Liang (Spicy Mixed Vegetable Soup).

Sugar (Nam Tan)

Sugar provides sweetness, one of the four basic flavours in Thai cooking. Thai desserts and sugar are inseparable. There are many types of sugar for sale in the markets. One type is caster sugar, which is either small grained or large grained. The purified type of sugar has finer grains and is often cheaper and more suitable for cooking in general. Another type of sugar is brown sugar. This is dark brown in colour and quite moist. It is ideal for hot coffee, cappuccino or even in ginger drinks to enhance the aroma. This sugar has more taste than caster sugar. Another type of sugar is made from coconut juice which is stored in a tin can, hence its nickname 'tinned sugar', or what Westerners know as palm sugar.

Tomato Ketchup (Sauce Ma-khue Thed)

Tomato sauce is used, as everywhere, to brighten up snacks, and is sometimes included as a curry ingredient. If you are bored with the bottled version, try making your own. All you need is a kilo of tomatoes, 5 onions, 5 red bird pepper chillies, a teaspoon of ground cinnamon, 2 cloves of garlic, 3 tablespoons of sugar, a teaspoon of salt, a cup of vinegar and two cups of water. Mix these ingredients together and boil until nearly over-cooked. Then pour into a blender and blend until smooth. Finally bring to a boil again to reduce.

Tofu (Tao-hoo)

Tofu is a vegetarian favourite which also takes its place in general cuisine because of its delicious taste. Tofu comes in varying grades—some soft, some hard—and is even available in tubes. The commonest, soft kind is called tao huay (bean junket). As well as being tasty, tofu contains 7.4 % protein, 3.5 % sugar, 2.7 % calcium plus phosphorous, iron and other vitamins. It is easy to digest and suitable for the elderly, whose digestive systems may be less efficient and whose teeth may be less strong. It is also low in cholesterol and perfect for people who are overweight or suffer from high blood pressure.

Vegetable Oil (Nam-man Pued)

In the past, Thai cooking often used pig fat but nowadays fear of cholesterol has popularized vegetable oils. Soya-bean oil is most commonly found, but maize, sunflower and other pressed oils will do just as well. During deep-frying, the temperature of the oil is 180-200 degrees Celsius, about double the heat of boiling water. Vegetables in particular cook quickly and retain more of their natural crispiness and flavour. But look out for splashes. During deep-frying, make sure the ingredients are dry, put them in carefully, and have a lid to cover the pan. Thais like to deep-fry sliced garlic to a crisp for sprinkling on noodles or adding to clear soups.

Vermicelli (Woon Sen)

There are various kinds of noodles, each one ideal for certain dishes. Rice noodles, for example, are good for making quick dishes such as Pork Guay Teow or Yen Ta Fo (Rice Noodles in Red Soup). Vermicelli is used to make salads most of the time. They are made from green beans and are hard and transparent. They are often wrapped and sold in bundles at the market. Be sure not to confuse them with rice noodles as they have a similar appearance. They must be left in cold or warm water to soften before preparing in any recipes.

Vinegar (Nam Som Sai-chu)

Thai vinegar is nearly always clear, perhaps because this avoids any confusion with the brown-coloured fish sauce. It is usually made from pineapple or other fruit and vegetables. In the past, Thais would always shake the bottle before buying to check for impurities, but nowadays reliable brands are available.

Vinegar is added to many dishes to add a splash of sourness. But its main place in Thai cuisine is on the table. Phrik Nam Som (Pickled Chillies in Vinegar) is one of the commonest condiments, especially popular with noodles and other dishes of Chinese origin.

White Soya Sauce (See-iew Khao)

White or light soya sauce is different from the darker version which is well known from Japanese food. It is a paler-brown colour and a lighter texture. It also has a finer, less salty taste. It is a main ingredient and condiment in Chinese cooking, especially with steamed dishes. It is now used often in Thai dishes too. Recently manufacturers have created interesting variants such as mushroom-flavoured white soya sauce, and soya sauce with iodine.

Wrapper Flour (Paeng Por Pia)

These are made from wheat flour, which is used to wrap up the ingredients. They are round, thin and bland tasting, so whatever ingredients are wrapped inside will have maximum flavour. They are used to make appetizers such as fresh spring rolls, fried spring rolls, or to wrap Indian desserts such as roti sai mai. There's another kind of wrapper called wonton wrapper. These are squared and slightly thicker than spring roll wrappers. They are yellow from the eggs they contain, and can be found at the oriental market.

Beef (Nuea Wua)

Thais consider beef a bit expensive and so a bit special. The most tender cuts come from the neck and the thighs, and these are good for dishes which are boiled, steamed, deep fried or stir-fried. The meat around the abdomen, chest and calves is not so tender and is used for stewing, making stock base and curries. The chest meat is so chewy that Thais call it 'crying tiger' but love it as an appetizer. Thai dishes never contain big chunks or slabs of beef. The meat is always cut into small pieces or thin slices. Partly this is simply economical. Partly it allows the meat to absorb the seasoning more thoroughly.

Chicken (Gai)

The second most famous Thai dish after Tom Yam Goong is Gai Yang & Khao Neow (Marinated Grilled Chicken with Sticky Rice). It is usually eaten with Som Tam (Papaya Salad) and some hot chilli sauce. Thais prefer the legs and thighs for this dish because these parts are chewier.

There is a common way of tenderizing the flesh. Just soak in lime juice for about thirty minutes. Like other kinds of meat, chicken contains protein and minerals, but is lower in fat and high in vitamin B1.

Crab (Poo)

Thais catch crabs from the rivers, the sea, and even from the paddy-fields. Poo na (field crabs) are freshwater crabs which are not so nutritious but make good pickles. Poo ma (horse crab) and Poo talay (sea crab or blue crab) are the commonest saltwater types. They have more nutritional value as well as a dose of iodine. You should buy crabs that are still alive. The males have more flesh than the females. The females have large breastplates which look like flower petals, and their shells echo if you knock on them.

Crispy Pork Skin (Kaep Moo)

Thai's who live in the north love to eat fattening food to protect them from the cold. Crispy Pork Skin eaten with nam phrik noom (grilled green chilli dip) is a favourite local snack as well as a souvenir for travelers. To make them, scrape off the fat from pork skin, leaving only a small amount of fat. Mix with salt, and dry in the sun. Cut into small pieces and deep fry in the oil over medium heat. When the pores on the skin start to expand, fry in boiling hot oil and scoop them out once the skin has fully expanded. Crispy Pork Skin are usually eaten with chilli paste dip. For those who are on a diet, the crispy pork skin without the fat are also available.

Freshwater Fish (Pla Nam Jued)

Nowadays, freshwater fish are also cultivated on fish farms. Thailand has hundreds of varieties of freshwater fish and virtually all are edible. The most popular are various kinds of catfish which live not only in the rivers but the paddy fields too. The snakehead fish can be fried, grilled or steamed.These and other kinds of freshwater fish can be used to make fish larb,the same recipe as Larb E-sarn (Spicy Northeastern-style Minced Pork Salad). When buying fresh fish, check that they have clear eyes, red gills and transparent scales. The flesh should be tight but not swollen up.

Jelly Fish (Mang Ga-prun)

When buying, you must look for the jellyfish which are as clear as chicken tendons, and do not have a foul smell. This will assure freshness. Spoiled ones will appear murky white in colour. You can always add jellyfish to yentafo as well as use them in other dishes, especially Thai salads. Yam woon sen(spice vermicelli salad), for example, are good when jellyfish is added to it. Chop the jellyfish into bite size pieces, boil and scatter on top of yam woonsen before serving.

Mackerel (Pla Two)

Mackerel is a type of sea fish. A well-known dish is fried mackerel served with shrimp paste or Nam Phrik Pla Two. To pick mackerel from the market for frying, select the fish that has been properly steamed. Normally, they are sold in a wooden steamer or a Kheng.

Another delicious mackerel dish is Tom Yam (Spicy Soup). It can be prepared similarly to Tom Yam Goong(Spicy Prawn Soup), but use mackerel instead of prawns. For Tom Yam, fresh mackerel can be used. Fresh mackerel should have clear eyes, red gills, white skin with a greenish glow, and does not have a bad smell. The flesh should be tight and should not swell when pressed.

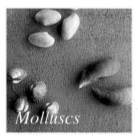

Molluscs (Hoy)

From the sea there are Hoy Ma-lang Phoo (mussels), Hoy Krang (cockles), Hoy Lai (a small cockle) and Hoy Nang-rom (oysters). From the rivers there are Hoy Khoeng (apple snails) and Hoy Khoem (pond snails). Almost any kind of mollusc makes a great Yam (Thai salad), and a great ingredient for a Tom Yam. Most types are delicious when boiled, stir-fried or grilled and eaten with a spicy sauce. Always buy them very fresh and preferably still alive. Storage is difficult because they go off easily. But if you want to keep them, they must first be boiled or steamed, then deshelled and kept in the fridge.

Northern Style Pork Sausage (Moo Yor)

Mostly, the storing method used is to make the food last longer. But the result of this has created accidental delicacies such as moo yor. It is a well known food of Esarn, and in the northern region. The method used in preparing them are similar to Western style sausages. This includes mincing pork, adding fish sauce, pepper, and a few other spices. The trick is to keep adding ice while mincing the pork so that the moo yor will be firm and chewy. Put the minced meat into thick banana leaves and tie tightly. Steam the minced meat and this will become moo yor. They are normally eaten in centimeter thick slices.

Pickled Pork Sausage (Naem)

Pickled pork sausage(naem) is another result of an accidental delicacy created through the preservation of food. To make naem, mix pork and skin with seasoning and wrap in banana leaves. Leave until they taste sour, squeezing some lime onto it to improve the taste. They are normally eaten as a snack while drinking alcohol. They can be served with roasted peanuts and fresh vegetables, whether it is coriander, cabbages or chillies. Naem can be deep-fried and are very delicious this way. Naem can also be put into fried rice using the same method that you make seafood fried rice. It is a favourite delicacy of all regions, but originated from the north and northeast.

Pork (Moo)

Pork is much more common than beef in Thai cooking. Minced pork is an ingredient in many dishes, often as a stuffing.The loin is the tenderest cut and this is preferred for dishes with grilled pork such as Khao Neow Moo Yang (Marinated Grilled Pork with Sticky Rice) and Moo Satay (Grilled Pork with Curry Peanut Sauce). Other cuts are used for deep-frying and stir-frying. Three layered pork is a cut with alternating layers of meat and fat, which is perfect for making crispy pork or the minced pork used in Gaeng Jued Pla Muek Yad Sai (Stuffed Squid Soup) and Gaeng Jued Ma-ra (Stuffed Chinese Bitter Gourd Soup) Pork contains high levels of vitamins B1, proteins and minerals.

Prawn (Goong)

Prawns come in many forms—saltwater or freshwater, natural or farmed—ranging in size from tiny to giant. The big ones include Goong mung-korn (dragon prawns) which have a hard grey shell and very white flesh, and Goong gula-dum (tiger prawns) which have blue shells and dense flesh which turns pink when cooked. Even bigger are the Goong gam-gram which are sometimes sold as 'lobsters'. But many believe the tastiest are the smaller ones, including the tiny river prawns best caught fresh and eaten deep-fried to a crisp. Prawns have as much protein as meat, but less vitamins and more potassium.

Sea Fish (Pla Thalay)

Fish is rich in protein like other kinds of meat. However, fish can be digested more easily. They also contain amino acids, digestible fat and a variety of vitamins. Fish oil contains vitamin A and D, while fish meat has plenty of vitamin B1, B2 and B6. Fish is extremely suitable for old people, children, and those who have high cholesterol or who may suffer from heart desease. To select saltwater fish from the market, check that the fish have clear eyes, red gills and no unsavoury smell. The flesh should be tight and should not swell when pressed. After the fish is gutted and cleaned, it should be kept in a freezer.

Squid (Pla Muek)

The two main types of squid used in Thai cooking are pla muek kluay (squid) and pla muek gra-dong (Cuttlefish). Pla muek kluay are round with little pouches on each side. Pla muek gra-dong are larger, flatter and white in colour. Both types have to be washed thoroughly to remove their filmy covering. Remove the innards, pull out the head, eyes, and cartilage, drain the ink, and make slits in the flesh so the seasoning will seep in. Rinse well under running water.

Experience Thai food in all its variety, learning traditional preparation and cooking methods, then savouring the spicy aromas and delightful flavours.

Gai Hor Bai Toey

Gai Yang & Khao Neow

Geow Tord

Gra-bong

Gra-thong Thong

Hoy Ma-lang Phoo Ob

Hoy Nang Rom Song Krueng

Khanom Pang Naa Moo

Khao Neow Moo Yang

Miang Som-O

Moo Satay

Naem Sod

Nam Phrik Noom & Kaep Moo

Pizza Tom Yam Goong

Pla Muek Ob Nei

Por Pia Tord

Sue Rong Hai

Tord Man Goong

INGREDIENTS

For 2 servings

For the chicken:

250g. (8 oz.)	chicken breast, cut into bite-size pieces
4 tsp.	white soya sauce
1/2 tbs.	sugar
4 tsp.	sesame oil
1/2 tbs.	whole black peppercorns
1/2 tsp.	salt
1 tbs.	garlic
8	strips of pandan leaf, cut 4cm. (1 1/2 inch) wide

For the sauce:

4 tsp.	dark soya sauce
1/2 tbs.	white soya sauce
1/2 tsp.	roasted sesame, slightly crushed
1 tsp.	sugar
1 tsp.	vinegar

Gai Hor Bai Toey
(Deep-fried Chicken in Pandan Leaves)

PREPARATION

In a mortar, pound together peppercorns and garlic until well blended.

In a mixing bowl, add the peppercorns and garlic mixture to the chicken.

Blend in white soya sauce, sugar and sesame oil until the ingredients are mixed well.

Marinate the chicken with the ingredients for approximately 1 hour.

Cut the marinated chicken into 8 pieces and wrap with the Pandan leaves, making a pyramidal shape.

Deep-fry in hot oil until cooked.

To make the sauce, mix the dark soya sauce and white soya sauce in a bowl.

Add sugar and vinegar. Stir well and sprinkle with sesame seeds.

Adjust the seasonings to obtain sweet and sour flavor as desired.

Serve with the sauce.

TIP Sauce for Chicken can be used as a substitute for the sauce in this recipe.

INGREDIENTS

For 4 servings

1	whole chicken, medium
1	whole lime
2 tbs.	garlic, finely chopped
2-3	coriander roots
1 tbs.	ground peppercorns
3/4 tbs.	salt
2 tbs.	white soya sauce
1 tbs.	dark soya sauce
1 tbs.	sugar
1 tbs.	whisky or brandy
1 tbs.	butter or margarine
For sticky rice:	
2 cups	sticky rice
3 cups	water

Gai Yang & Khao Neow
(Marinated Grilled Chicken with Sticky Rice)

PREPARATION

Cut the chicken into halves. Clean and remove the insides. Rub the chicken pieces all over with lime.

In a mortar, pound garlic, galangal, coriander roots, and peppercorns until mixed well. Then, add salt, white soya sauce, dark soya sauce, sugar, and whisky. Mix thoroughly.

Marinate the chicken with the mixture from step 2 for 1 hour.

Charcoal grill the chicken until cooked. Occasionally brush butter over the chicken.

To steam the sticky rice, soak the rice in water for 3-5 hours (or overnight). Rinse and drain well.

Line the perforated part of a steamer with a white thin cloth. Place the sticky rice on the cloth and wrap.

Put water in the bottom of the steamer, and steam the rice for approximately 30 minutes over moderate heat. Remove when the rice has cooked. Well cooked rice should look dry and soft when it is pressed flat.

When serving, serve with steamed sticky rice, Sauce for Chicken, and Nam Jim Jaew (Northeastern-style Spicy Sauce).

TIP "Gai Yang" can also be grilled or roasted. Roasted chicken is more moist then grilled chicken.

INGREDIENTS

For 2-4 servings

10-15	wonton wrappers
200g. (7 oz.)	minced pork
2 tsp.	coriander root, finely chopped
2 tsp.	garlic, finely chopped
1/2 tsp.	salt
2 cups	vegetable oil

(Crispy Wonton)

PREPARATION

Using a mortar, pound the coriander root and garlic until finely blended. Mix with pork and salt in a mixing bowl.

Place a wonton wrapper on your palm and put a teaspoon of pork in the center. Wrap the pork. If the wonton does not seal well, use egg yolk to help seal the wrapper.

Deep fry in hot oil for 3-5 minutes until golden. Drain on paper to absorb the excess fat.

Serve with Chinese Plum Sauce, Sauce for Chicken or Ar-jad.

TIP This dish derived from a popular Chinese appetizer or "dim-sum".

INGREDIENTS

For 2 servings

250 g. (8 oz.)	mature pumpkin, peeled and cut into short matchstick-size pieces
1 tbs.	lime juice
1/2 cup	coconut milk
150 g. (5 1/2 oz.)	multi-purpose flour
2 cups	vegetable oil
1/2 tbs.	garlic, finely chopped
1/2 tbs.	coriander root, finely chopped
1/2 tbs.	whole white peppercorns
1 tsp.	white soya sauce
1 tsp.	sugar

Gra-bong
(Crispy Pumpkin)

PREPARATION

In a large bowl, mix the lime juice with 2 cups of cold water. Put the pumpkin into a bowl to wash, and then drain.

Using a mortar, grind the garlic, coriander roots and peppercorns. Set aside.

In a mixing bowl, mix together multi-purpose flour, white soya sauce, and sugar. Gradually, add coconut milk to the mixture. Knead until blended well.

Add the garlic and peppercorns mixture into the batter. Blend until the batter is thick enough to coat the pumpkin. If the batter becomes too thick, add more coconut milk.

Coat the pumpkin in the mixed batter.

Put oil in a deep-frying pan over moderate heat. Then, deep-fry 5-6 pieces at a time until golden and crispy.

Place the crispy pumpkin on absorbent paper.

Serve with Ar-jad (Cucumber Sauce) or Chinese Plum Sauce .

TIP Pumpkin can be substituted by green papaya, banana buds, mushroom and gourd.

INGREDIENTS

For 20 cups

For crispy cup:

250 g. (8 oz.)	multi-purpose flour
1/2 tsp.	salt
1	egg
1 cup	water
1/4 tsp.	baking soda (optional)
1	mould (typical mould for "Grathong Thong")

For the filling:

2 tbs.	corn oil
4 tbs.	onion, finely chopped
200 g. (7 oz.)	chicken or pork, finely minced
1/4 cup	sweet corn
2 tbs.	carrot, finely diced
2 tbs.	sugar
2 tbs.	white soya sauce
1/2 tsp.	salt
1/2 tsp.	ground black peppercorns
2 tsp.	curry powder
	coriander leaves and finely sliced red fresh chilli, for garnishing

Gra-thong Thong

(Crispy Cup with Minced Chicken)

PREPARATION

To make the crispy cups: mix the flour, salt, egg, water, and baking soda in a mixing bowl. Whisk until finely blended. This should become a thick, creamy batter. Allow to rest for 1 hour.

Heat the oil in a deep frying pan, and dip the mould in the hot oil to heat it up. If the oil is not hot enough, the batter will not stick to the mould when dipped. Then, dip the outside of the hot mould into the batter. Make sure that only the outside surface is covered with the batter. Put the batter-covered mould immediately back into the hot oil. The cup should be cooked for about 20 seconds so it can be detached from the mould.

Remove the mould and continue to fry the cup until golden and crispy. Then, remove the cup(s) from the pan and drain on absorbant paper. Repeat until the batter is finished.

To make the filling, heat the oil in a pan, and stir fry the onions and chicken for 2 minutes.

Add sweet corn, carrots, sugar, white soya sauce, and salt. Stir fry for 30 seconds. Add ground peppercorns and curry powder, and stir for another 20 seconds.

Allow the filling to cool before filling the crispy cups. Garnish each filled cup with coriander leaves and red fresh chilli strips.

TIP Vol-au-vent cases can be used instead of the "Gra-thong Thong." The crispy cups can be stored in an air-tight container for 2 weeks.

(Steamed Mussels with Herbs)

PREPARATION

Place the mussels in a steamer over boiling water and sprinkle with basil leaves, kaffir lime leaves, lemongrass, garlic, and shallot. Steam for 10 minutes.

Remove from the heat and wait for a few minutes before opening the steamer. This is to let the herbs flavor the mussels.

TIP Accompanied with Nam Jim Thalay (Spicy Seafood Sauce)

INGREDIENTS

For 4 servings

2 kg. (4 1/2 lb.)	mussels, cleaned well
1 cup	sweet basil leaves
3 tbs.	kaffir lime leaves
3 tbs.	lemongrass, sliced into strips
3 tbs.	garlic, finely chopped
2 tbs.	shallot, finely chopped

INGREDIENTS

For 2-4 servings

8-10	fresh oyster, cleaned well
1/2 cup	Grathin
2 tbs.	shallot, finely chopped
4-5	lime or lemon, cut into pieces
2 tbs.	vegetable oil
3 tbs.	chilli sauce

(Savoury Fresh Oysters)

PREPARATION

In a frying pan, heat the oil. Then, saute the shallot in the hot oil until golden and crispy. Then, remove all the oil. Set aside the crispy shallot

On a serving platter, arrange the grathin, lime and crispy shallot into separate piles. Then, place the oysters back into their shells for serving. Accompany with a small dish of chilli sauce.

To eat, put the oysters into individual spoons and with a squeeze of lime on top. Then, top with grathin, crispy shallot and chilli sauce.

TIP The grathin adds a natural sweetness to this dish.

(Deep-fried Minced Pork Toast)

PREPARATION

In a mixing bowl, mix together the minced pork, egg, white soya sauce, coriander roots, and peppercorns.

On each piece of bread, place some pork mixture in the center.

In a deep frying pan, heat the oil. Deep fry the bread in the hot oil until golden.

When serving, garnish with coriander leaf and fresh chillies.

TIP Usually accompanied with Ar-jad. (Cucumber Sauce)

INGREDIENTS

For 4 servings

4	slices of bread, cut into 4 pieces
200 g. (7 oz.)	minced pork
1	egg
1 1/2 tbs.	white soya sauce
1 tbs.	coriander roots, pounded
1/2 tsp.	ground peppercorns
2 cups	vegeatble oil
	coriander leaves and red fresh chillies for garnishing.

INGREDIENTS

For 2 servings

300 g. (10 1/2 oz.)	pork, sliced
1 tbs.	garlic, finely chopped
2	coriander roots
1/2 tsp.	ground peppercorns
1 1/2 tsp.	fish sauce
1 1/2 tbs.	white soya sauce
1 tsp.	sugar
For sticky rice	
1 cup	sticky rice
1 1/2 cup	water

Khao Neow Moo Yang
(Marinated Grilled Pork with Sticky Rice)

PREPARATION

In a mortar, pound garlic, coriander roots, and peppercorns. Mix well and place in a mixing bowl.

In the mixing bowl with the garlic mixture, add fish sauce, white soya sauce, and sugar. Mix well. Marinate the pork in this mixture for 1 hour.

Charcoal grill the pork until cooked.

To steam the sticky rice, soak the sticky rice in water for 3-5 hours (or overnight). Rinse and drain well.

Line the perforated part of a steamer with a white thin cloth. Place the sticky rice on the cloth and wrap.

Put water in the bottom of the steamer and steam the rice for approximately 20 minutes over moderate heat. Remove when rice has cooked. Cooked rice should look dry and soft when it is pressed flat.

Serve with Nam Jim Jaew. (Northeastern-style spicy sauce)

TIP This dish is one of the most favourite and common Thai hawker food.

INGREDIENTS

For 2 servings

200 g. (7 oz.)	pomelo
2 tbs.	young ginger, cut into small dices
2 tbs.	cashew nuts, roasted
2 tbs.	peanuts, roasted
2 tbs.	shallots, thinly sliced or diced
2 tbs.	lime, thinly sliced or diced
6	fresh chilies or dried chilies

Miang Som-O
(Pomelo Savouries)

PREPARATION

Arrange all ingredients on a large serving platter in separate piles.

To eat, spoon each filling onto an individual plate. Toss thoroughly.

TIP Sometimes the dish can be served with crispy rice crackers or wrapping leaves. The common wrapping leaves are young lettuce and wild pepper leaves . To eat, spoon each filling onto the leaf, and wrap it up.

INGREDIENTS

For 4-6 servings

500 g. (1 lb.)	pork, sliced thinly 2.5 cm. X 10 cm. (1" X 4")
1 1/2 tbs.	lemongrass, finely chopped
1 tbs.	galangal, finely chopped
2 tbs.	shallot, finely chopped
1 1/2 tbs.	garlic, finely chopped
2 tbs.	brown coriander seeds, pounded
1 tbs.	curry powder
1 tbs.	kaffir lime leaves, finely chopped
2 1/2 tbs.	sugar
1/2 tsp.	salt
3/4 cup	coconut milk, boiled
40	satay sticks or skewers

Moo Satay

(Grilled Pork with Curry Peanut Sauce)

PREPARATION

In a mortar, pound lemongrass, galangal, shallot, garlic, coriander seeds, kaffir lime leaves, curry powder, sugar, and salt together. Mix well.

Marinate the pork in the mixture for 20 minutes. Thread the pork onto the satay sticks.

Charcoal grill the pork. Use a brush to apply the coconut milk to the pork while grilling.

Serve with Nam Jim Moo Satay (Curry Peanut Sauce) and Ar-jad (Cucumber Sauce).

TIP Pork can be substituted with chicken or beef.

Naem Sod
(Spicy Minced Pork Salad)

PREPARATION

In a mixing bowl, mix the minced pork, pork skin, ginger, shallots and fresh chillies together. Toss until mixed well.

Season with lime juice, fish sauce, sugar and chilli powder.

When serving, sprinkle with roast peanuts, coriander leaves and spring onion.

TIP Usually accompanied with fresh vegetables as side dishes, e.g. cabbage and coriander.

INGREDIENTS

For 2 servings

1 1/2 cups	minced pork, boiled
1/2 cup	pork skin, boiled and cut into small pieces
1/4 cup	young ginger, finely chopped
4	shallots, finely chopped
4	fresh chillies, finely chopped
1 tbs.	lime juice
1 tsp.	fish sauce
1/4 tsp.	sugar
2 tbs.	roast peanuts
1/2 tsp.	chilli powder
	coriander leaves and chopped spring onion for garnishing

INGREDIENTS

For 2 servings

3	large green chillies
1/4 cup	eggplant, finely sliced
1/2 tbs.	garlic, chopped
1 tsp.	shallot, chopped
1 1/2 tbs.	fish sauce
1 1/2 tbs.	lime juice
1/2 tsp.	sugar
1 cup	crispy pork skin, for side dish

(Grillled Green Chilli Dip & Crispy Pork Skin)

PREPARATION

Grill the green chillies, eggplant, garlic and shallot over moderate heat until the eggplant's skin becomes dark and the inside becomes soft. Remove the dark skin.

In a mortar, pound the green chillies, eggplant, garlic and shallot until thoroughly mixed together.

Add fish sauce, lime juice, sugar and boiled water to the mixture.

Serve with crispy pork skin and boiled vegetables such as white greens, pumpkin, baby-corn and fresh cucumber.

TIP Eggplant is added to balance the strong hot taste of chillies.

Por Pia Tord
(Deep-fried Spring Rolls)

PREPARATION

In a mortar, pound together the coriander roots, garlic, and peppercorns. Set aside.

In a pan, fry the minced pork, minced prawns, and Chinese mushrooms with the garlic mixture from step 1. Season with white soya sauce and sugar. Add vermicelli and shredded cabbage. Stir-fry until cooked. This becomes the filling.

On a flat and smooth surface, spread a flour wrapper. Place some of the filling on the center of each wrapper. Fold the top and bottom edge to cover the filling. Fold the right side and roll until the wrapper completely covers the filling. The spring roll should look like a 8 cm. (3 inch) sausage.

Heat the oil in a deep-frying pan over moderate heat. Deep-fry each spring roll for 4-5 minutes until golden. Remove and drain well on absorbent papers. Do not put more than 3-4 spring rolls in a frying pan at a time.

Serve with Chinese Plum Sauce and fresh vegetables such as sweet basil leaves and cucumber slices.

TIP To seal the wrapper well, brush the wrapper edges with a beaten egg.

INGREDIENTS

For 8 servings

100 g. (3 1/2 oz.)	vermicelli, soak in water until soft and cut into 2.5 cm. (1 inch) long pieces
20 g. (3/4 oz.)	Chinese mushrooms, sliced into small pieces
150 g. (5 1/2 oz.)	minced pork
100 g. (3 1/2 oz.)	prawns, peel and remove the head and tail, and then mince
1 cup	cabbage, shredded
1 tsp.	coriander root, finely chopped
1 tsp.	garlic, finely chopped
1 tsp.	ground peppercorns
1 1/2 tbs.	white soya sauce
1/2 tbs.	sugar
15	flour wrappers
1 cup	vegetable oil

INGREDIENTS

For 6-8 servings

1 loaf	French bread, thinly sliced
20	small prawns, boiled
2	squid, boiled and cut into small pieces
200 g. (7 oz.)	straw mushrooms, boiled and cut into small pieces
2 tbs.	instant "tom yam" paste
2 tbs.	lime juice
2 tbs.	fish sauce
1 tbs.	sugar
1/2 cup	coriander leaves
1/2 cup	red fresh chillies, cut into strips
4	kaffir lime leaves, thinly chopped
1/2 cup	mayonnaise

Pizza Tom Yam Goong
(Spicy Prawn Pizza)

PREPARATION

In a small mixing bowl, mix together instant "tom yam" paste, lime juice, fish sauce, and sugar.

Spread the "tom yam" mixture on each slice of bread. Top with pieces of prawn, squid, mushroom, kaffir lime leaves, coriander leaves, fresh chillies, and a little mayonnaise.

Bake at 400° F until golden and crispy.

TIP Instant "tom yam" paste is available in various oriental grocery stores.

Pla Muek Ob Nei
(Butter Baked Squid)

PREPARATION

Rinse the squid well; remove the insides and drain.

In an oven, bake the squid until thoroughly cooked. Occasionally brush the squid with butter or margarine.

Garnish with slices of spring onion, lime and garlic. Season with peppercorns.

TIP Usually serve with Nam Jim Thalay (Spicy Seafood Sauce)

INGREDIENTS

For 2 servings

1	fresh squid
2 tbs.	butter/margarine
	spring onion, lime,
	garlic and whole black
	peppercorns for garnishing

Sue Rong Hai
(Marinated Grilled Beef with Northeastern-style Spicy Sauce)

PREPARATION

Marinate the beef with fish sauce, white soya sauce, sugar and brandy for 1 hour.

Charcoal grill for approximately 8 minutes or until the beef becomes medium rare.

Serve with Nam Jim Jaew. (Northeastern-style Spicy Sauce)

TIP The name means "Crying Tiger". This is one of the hottest dish of Esarn.

INGREDIENTS

300 g. (10 1/2 oz.)	beef (sirloin), sliced
1 tsp.	fish sauce
1 tbs.	white soya sauce
1 tsp.	sugar
2 tsp.	brandy (optional)

Tord Man Goong
(Deep-fried Prawn Cake)

PREPARATION

Clean the prawns well. Peel the shell off and devein. Chop them finely.

Mix the prawns with salt and peppercorn. Knead with rolling-pin until the prawn mixture becomes smooth and elastic.

Take a tablespoon of the prawn mixture between the palms of your hand and shape into balls. Press the prawn balls with a spoon slightly. Then, roll in the bread crumbs.

Heat the oil in the frying pan using high heat, and fry until both sides of the prawn-ball become golden.

TIP Usually serve with Chinese Plum Sauce.

INGREDIENTS

For 4 servings

500g. (1 lb.)	prawns
1/2 cup	bread crumbs
1/2 tsp.	salt
1/8 tsp.	ground peppercorns
2 cups	vegetable oil

Gaeng Aom

Gaeng Ga-ree Gai

Gaeng Hoh

Gaeng Hung Lay

Gaeng Jued Ma-ra

Gaeng Jued Pla Muek Yad Sai

Gaeng Kae

Gaeng Khiew Wan Gai

Gaeng Khua Sup-pa-rod

Gaeng Liang

Gaeng Lueng

Gaeng Som

Gaeng Tai Pla

Gai Toon Hed Hom

Goong Ga-thi Nor Mai Sod

Jaew Hon

Khai Phalo

Mussamun Nuea

Phak Gad Jor

Phanaeng Moo

Poh Taek

Tom Kha Gai

Tom Krueng Nai

Tom Yam Goong

INGREDIENTS

For 2 servings

300 g. (10 1/2 oz.)	pork fillet, sliced
2 tbs.	instant red curry paste
2 cups	coconut milk
4	dried chillies
10	sweet basil leaves
4 slices	galangal
4-5	kaffir lime leaves
1 tsp.	lemongrass, finely chopped
2 tsp.	fish sauce
1 tsp.	sugar

Gaeng Aom
(Curry of Pork and Innards)

PREPARATION

In a pot, bring 1 cup of the coconut milk to a boil. Add instant red curry paste. Stir-fry for a few minutes. Add pork and stir-fry.

Add the rest of the coconut milk, dried chillies, sweet basil leaves, galangal, kaffir lime leaves, and lemongrass. Simmer until cooked.

Season with fish sauce and sugar. Remove from heat.

When serving, top with dried chillies or fresh chillies.

TIP Sometimes, bitter gourd is added to the dish.

INGREDIENTS

For 2 servings

300 g. (10 1/2 oz.)	chicken, cleaned and cut into pieces
2 cups	coconut milk
3 tbs.	instant yellow curry paste
2	potatoes, peeled and cut into bite-size pieces
4-5	cardamom leaves
1 tbs.	fish sauce
1/2 tbs	sugar
1 cup	water

Gaeng Ga-ree Gai
(Yellow Chicken Curry)

PREPARATION

In a pot, fry the instant yellow curry paste with the coconut milk until boiling. Add chicken and water. Simmer over low heat until the chicken becomes tender.

Add potatoes, and season with fish sauce, sugar and cardamom leaves. Simmer until chicken and potatoes become soft. Adjust the taste before removing from heat.

When serving, accompanied with Ar-jad (Cucumber Sauce) and sprinkle with crispy shallots.

TIP Add some water if the curry becomes too dry while simmering.

INGREDIENTS

For 2 servings

70 g. (2 oz.)	pork
100 g. (3 1/2 oz.)	vermicelli, soak in water until soft
2 tbs.	instant hung lay curry paste
1 tsp.	shrimp paste
5	dried chillies
2 tsp.	shallots, finely chopped
2 tsp.	garlic, finely chopped
1 tsp.	lemongrass, finely chopped
4 slices	galangal
6	kaffir lime leaves
2-3	crisp eggplants, cut into quarters
1/4 cup	long beans, cut into 2 cm. (1 inch) long pieces
30 g. (1 oz.)	pickled bamboo shoots, cut into small pieces
20 g. (3/4 oz.)	pickled cabbage, shredded
2 tbs.	tamarind juice
1 1/2 tsp.	palm sugar
1 tsp.	dark soya sauce

Gaeng Hoh
(Dried Northern-style Mixed Curry)

PREPARATION

In a mortar, pound dried chillies, shallot, garlic and shrimp paste together until blended well.

In a frying pan, heat the oil and stir-fry the instant hung lay curry paste with the chillies mixture (from step 1) lemongrass, galangal, kaffir lime leaves and pork until the pork is cooked.

Add crisp eggplants and long beans, stir-fry until they become soft. Then, add bamboo shoot and pickled cabbage. Stir-fry.

Season with tamarind juice, palm sugar and dark soya sauce. Add vermicelli and stir-fry until all mixed well. Remove.

TIP "Gaeng Hoh" means "mix all together". The dish consists of almost all common ingredients of northern dishes stir-fried together.

INGREDIENTS

For 2 servings

1 1/2 cups	pork, diced
3 tbs.	instant hung lay curry paste
1 1/2 tbs.	thin-sliced ginger
1/4 cup	roasted peanuts
1 tbs.	garlic, pounded
2 tbs.	fish sauce
1 tbs.	sugar
1 tbs.	tamarind juice
3 cups	water

Gaeng Hung Lay
(Northern-style Pork Curry)

PREPARATION

Marinate pork with hung lay curry paste for 20 minutes.

Put marinated pork in a pot and add water. Simmer until tender.

Add ginger slices, peanuts and garlic. Simmer well.

Flavor with fish sauce, sugar and tamarind juice. Simmer until the curry becomes slightly thick.

When serving, garnish with thin-sliced ginger.

TIP This dish originated in Burma. It is considered to be an elegant dish for special occasions such as celebrations or welcoming parties.

(Stuffed Chinese Bitter Gourd Soup)

PREPARATION

Cut Chinese bitter gourd into 5 cm. (2-inch) pieces. Take out the seeds.

Using a mortar, pound the coriander roots, garlic and peppercorns together. Mix with the pork and egg white.

Stuff the Chinese bitter gourd with the pork mixture.

Boil the pork stock. Put in the stuffed bitter gourd. Season with white soya sauce. Simmer over low heat until pork is done.

When serving, put 2 stuffed bitter gourds in a serving dish and pour the pork soup over them. Garnish with coriander leaves and peppercorns.

TIP To reduce bitter taste, soak the bitter gourd in salt water overnight. (For each cup of water, use 1 teaspoon of salt.)

INGREDIENTS

For 2 servings

1	Chinese bitter gourd
150g. (5 1/2 oz.)	minced pork
1	egg
2	coriander roots
1 tbs.	garlic, finely chopped
1/2 tsp.	peppercorns
2 tbs.	white soya sauce
2 cups	pork stock
	coriander leaves and peppercorns , for garnishing.

Gaeng Jued Pla Muek Yad Sai
(Stuffed Squid Soup)

INGREDIENTS

For 2 servings

200g. (7 oz.)	squid
100g. (3 1/2 oz.)	minced pork
2-3	coriander roots
1 tbs.	garlic, finely chopped
1/2 tsp.	whole black peppercorns
1 tbs.	fish sauce
5 cups	pork stock
2 tbs.	white soya sauce
	spring onion and diced
	carrots, for garnishing

PREPARATION

Remove the squid head, insides, and transparent bones; cut the tentacles from the head. Rinse the squid well and drain.

Using a mortar, finely pound the coriander roots, chopped garlic and peppercorn together. Mix thoroughly.

Mix the minced pork with the mixture from Step 2 and add 1 tablespoon of white soya sauce. Marinate for about 20 minutes. This becomes the filling.

Stuff each squid with the filling until approximately 3/4 full.

Bring the pork stock to a boil. Put the stuffed squids into the boiling soup for 10-15 minutes or until the pork is done.

Season with fish sauce, white soya sauce, and ground peppercorns.

When serving, garnish with sliced spring onion and diced carrots.

TIP For "Gaeng Jued" (Thai clear soup), salt can be used instead of fish sauce. Fish sauce will give a slight fish odor.

INGREDIENTS

For 4 servings

1	whole freshwater fish, medium-size, grilled
5	crisp eggplants, cut into halves
1 tbs.	long beans, cut into 5-cm. (2-inch) long pieces
1 tbs.	acacia, cut into 2.5-cm. (1-inch) long pieces
1 tbs.	morning glory, cut into 2.5-cm. (1 inch) long pieces
1 tbs.	sawtooth coriander, cut into 5 cm. (2 inch) long pieces
2 slices	galangal
1 tbs.	lemongrass, cut into 2.5-cm. (1 inch) long pieces
1 tbs.	shallot
1 tbs.	garlic
2 tbs.	bamboo shoots, cut into 2.5-cm. (1 inch) long pieces
1	galingale root
2	red fresh chillies
1 tbs.	sweet basil leaves
1 tsp.	fish sauce
3 cups	water

Gaeng Kae
(Spicy Northern-style Vegetable Soup)

PREPARATION

In a mortar, pound together the galangal, lemongrass, shallot and garlic. This creates the herb mixture.

Using a food blender, blend the flesh of the fish with half of the herb mixture.

Bring the water to a boil, and add the remaining herb mixture and blended fish. Boil for 3-5 minutes.

Put all of the vegetables into the soup. Finally add sweet basil leaves. Boil for another 5 minutes.

Taste the soup, and add fish sauce if desired.

TIP This northern dish is suitable for those weight-watchers.

PREPARATION

Using a frying pan, fry green curry paste with half of the coconut milk using low heat. Add chicken and stir-fry until the chicken is throughly cooked.

Add the remaining coconut milk, water and crisp eggplants. Bring to a boil.

Season with fish sauce, sugar, sweet basil leaves, and red chillies. Quickly remove from heat.

TIP The longer the curry is left over the heat, the drier the curry will become. Add some water if the curry appears too dry.

INGREDIENTS

For 2 servings

250g. (8 oz.)	chicken breast, sliced
3 tbs.	instant green curry paste
1 cup	coconut milk
4	crisp eggplants, cut into quarters
1/4 cup	sweet basil leaves
4	red chillies, sliced
2 tbs.	fish sauce
1 tbs.	sugar
1/2 cup	water

(Red Curry with Pineapple)

PREPARATION

In a pot, stir-fry 1/2 cup of coconut milk with red curry paste until the coconut milk is boiling.

Add the remaining coconut milk, chicken, pineapple and dried shrimps. Simmer over moderate heat until all cooked.

Season with fish sauce and palm sugar. Stir well and remove from heat.

TIP Prawns can be used instead of chicken. Also, if the pineapple is too sour, pour some lime juice and salt over the pinapple. Let it stand for 20 minutes. This should help reducing the strong sour taste of the pineapple.

INGREDIENTS

For 2 servings

300g.(10 1/2 oz.)	chicken, cut into bite-size pieces
2 cups	pineapple, cut into bite-size pieces
3 tbs.	dried shrimps, pounded
3 tbs.	instant red curry paste
2 1/2 cups	coconut milk
2 1/2 tbs.	fish sauce
2 tsp.	palm sugar

INGREDIENTS

For 2 servings

1/2 cup	fillet of freshwater fish, grilled
1/2 cup	sweet basil leaves
50 g. (1 1/2 oz.)	baby-corn, cut into halves
50 g. (1 1/2 oz.)	straw mushrooms, cut into halves
50 g. (1 1/2 oz.)	pumpkin, cut into bite-size pieces
50 g. (1 1/2 oz.)	angled gourd, cut into bite-size pieces
5	shallots, finely chopped
1 tsp.	shrimp paste
1 tsp.	whole black peppercorns
2 cups	chicken stock
1 tbs.	fish sauce

Gaeng Liang
(Spicy Mixed Vegetable Soup)

PREPARATION

In a food processor, blend the grilled freshwater fish fillets, shallots, shrimp paste and peppercorns together. Remove. This is the soup paste.

In a pot, bring the chicken stock to the boil. Add the soup paste, pumpkin, baby-corns, angled gourd and mushrooms. Bring to the boil once again.

Season with fish sauce and add sweet basil leaves. Stir well and remove from heat.

TIP Boiled prawns can also be added to the soup.

PREPARATION

In a mortar, pound the dried chillies, turmeric, garlic, and shallot until they are mixed well. Then, add the mackerel and shrimp paste. Pound until blended. This creates the spicy paste.

In a pot, mix water with the spicy paste. Then, bring to a boil. When the soup is vigorously boiling, add the coconut shoot.

Season with fish sauce, sugar and tamarind juice. Bring the soup to a boil once again using high heat. Then, remove from heat.

TIP The name of this particular dish means "Yellow Soup" because of its colour. The yellow colour comes naturally from turmeric.

INGREDIENTS

For 2 servings

2 tbs.	mackerel, grilled with head and bones removed
1 cup	coconut shoot, cut into small dices
6	dried chillies
1 tsp.	turmeric, finely chopped
2 tsp.	garlic, finely chopped
2 tsp.	shallot, finely chopped
1 tsp.	shrimp paste
1 cup	water
2 tbs.	fish sauce
1/2 tbs.	sugar
3 tbs.	tamarind juice

INGREDIENTS

For 2 servings

400g. (15 oz.)	prawns or fish fillets
3 cups	water
125g. (4 1/2 oz.)	straw mushrooms
1/2 cup	green papaya, peeled and cut into medium-sized pieces
3	dried chillies, soaked until soft
2 tsp.	galingale, finely chopped (optional)
2 tsp.	garlic, finely chopped
2 tsp.	shallots, finely chopped
4 tbs.	tamarind juice
2 tbs.	lime juice (optional)
1 tbs.	palm sugar, chopped
1 tsp.	salt

Gaeng Som
(Spicy and Sour Green Papaya Soup)

PREPARATION

Simmer the prawns or fish fillets in 3 cups of water until thoroughly cooked. Let cool, then peel the prawns or remove any bones from the fish. Set aside the remaining stock. Reserve one fish fillet for garnishing.

In a mortar, pound the prawns or fish until well mashed. Set aside. A food-processor can be used instead of the mortar.

In a mortar, pound the dried chillies, galingale, garlic and shallots until blended well. This creates the spice paste.

In a pot, boil the reserved stock, prawns or fish , spice paste and papaya together. Simmer until thoroughly cooked.

To add flavor, use tamarind juice, lime juice, palm sugar and salt.

When serving, garnish with chillies and place a fish fillet on top.

TIP Lime juice is a substitute for tamarind juice. However, the soup will be slightly clearer.

(Spicy Fish Entrails Soup)

INGREDIENTS

For 2 servings

For Tai Pla Paste:

10	dried chillies
1 1/2 tbs.	fresh chillies
1 tsp.	galangal, finely chopped
1 stalk	lemongrass, finely chopped
1 tbs.	kaffir lime skin, finely chopped
1 tbs.	shallot, finely chopped
2 tbs.	garlic, finely chopped
1 tsp.	turmeric, finely chopped
2 tsp.	shrimp paste
1 tsp.	salt

For Vegetables:

1/4 cup	long beans, cut into 1-cm. (1/2-inch) pieces
1/4 cup	pumpkin, cut into bite size pieces
4	crisp eggplants
4	kaffir lime leaves

For the soup :

3 tbs.	fish maw
1 1/2 cup	water
100 g. (3 1/2 oz.)	mackerel, grilled with head and bones removed
1 tbs.	tamarind juice
1 tsp.	palm sugar

PREPARATION

In a mortar, pound together all the Tai Pla paste ingredients.

Using a pot, boil water with fish maw. Then, strain. Add the paste mixture (from step 1) into the soup. Cover and bring to a boil.

Add the grilled mackerel, tamarind juice and sugar. Adjust the taste if desired. Then put all the vegetables into the soup. Simmer until cooked.

TIP   This is a typical southern dish which contains approximately 350 calories.

Gai Toon Hed Hom
(Chicken Soup with Dried Mushroom)

PREPARATION

Rinse chicken well and drain. Cut off the head and feet. Place the chicken in a pot or a pressure-cooker and pour in water to cover the chicken.

Add ginger, salt, white soya sauce, peppercorns and 3 stalks of spring onion to the soup. Cook the chicken until it becomes tender. Adjust the seasoning to taste.

Rinse the mushrooms well. Put into the pot and bring to a boil.

To serve, sprinkle with whole black peppercorns.

TIP Good dried mushrooms usually come from China.

INGREDIENTS

For 2 servings

1	whole chicken, small size
10	dried mushrooms, soaked in warm water until soft
1	slice of ginger, slightly pounded.
2 tsp.	salt
1 tbs.	whole black peppercorns
2 tbs.	white soya sauce
3 stalks	spring onion

(Prawns and Bamboo Shoot In Coconut Soup)

PREPARATION

In a pot, bring the coconut milk to a boil. Add prawns and water. Simmer for 5 minutes.

Add twisted cluster beans and bamboo shoots.

Season with fish sauce, sugar, and shrimp paste.

TIP Bamboo shoots can be substituted with coconut shoots.

INGREDIENTS

For 2 servings

4-6	prawns, clean well and remove back vein
100 g. (3 1/2 oz.)	bamboo shoots, cut into 5-cm (2-inch) long pieces
1/2 cup	coconut milk
50 g. (1 1/2 oz.)	twisted cluster beans, remove pods
1 tbs.	shrimp paste
1 tbs.	fish sauce
1/2 tbs.	sugar
2 cups	water

INGREDIENTS

For 2 servings

200 g. (7 oz.)	beef, thinly sliced
200 g. (7 oz.)	beef entrails, cut into pieces (optional)
50 g. (2 oz.)	vermicelli, soaked in water until soft
5 cups	beef stock
1	egg
1/2 cup	morning glory, cut into 2-inch (5-cm.) long pieces
15	sweet basil leaves
1/4	cabbage
3	small tomatoes
1 stalk	lemongrass, cut into 1-inch (2.5-cm.) long pieces
3 slices	galangal, grilled
5	kaffir lime leaves
1 tbs.	fish sauce

Jaew Hon
(Northeastern-style Spicy Soup)

PREPARATION

In a large pot, heat the beef stock. Then, add lemongrass, galangal, kaffir lime leaves and fish sauce. Bring to a boil.

When serving, arrange all the ingredients on a serving plate. For the soup, serve in a sukiyaki pot or a stew pot on a portable stove to keep the soup boiling constantly.

To eat, pick any desired ingredients and put them into the boiling soup. Then, remove to individual's dish when cooked. Accompanied with Nam Jim Jaew (Northeastern-style Spicy Sauce)

TIP This dish is also called "Northeastern-style Sukiyaki", since the serving style is similar to the Japanese sukiyaki. However, the differences lie in the northeastern-style soup and the sauce.

INGREDIENTS

For 2-4 servings

300 g. (10 1/2 oz.)	pork, cut into bite-size pieces
5	eggs, boiled
1	tofu cake, cut into bite-size pieces
2	coriander roots
1 tsp.	garlic, finely chopped
1 tbs.	five spices powder
1 tsp.	whole black peppercorns
2 tbs.	palm sugar
1 tsp.	black soya sauce
2 tbs.	fish sauce
4 cups	water

(Boiled Eggs with Five Spices Soup)

PREPARATION

In a mortar, pound together coriander roots, garlic, and black peppercorns.

In a pot, brown the pork with the mixture from step 1. Add eggs, tofu, five spices powder, and water.

Season with palm sugar , fish sauce and black soya sauce. There should be a sweet taste.

Simmer for 1 hour.

TIP Instant "Phalo Powder" is also available at various oriental grocery stores.

INGREDIENTS

For 2 servings

500 g. (1 lb.)	beef
2 cup	coconut milk
3	potatoes, peeled and cut into bite-size pieces
1	onion, cut into quarters
2 tbs.	instant mussamun curry paste
2 tbs.	fish sauce
2 tsp.	sugar
1/4 cup	roasted peanuts
1/4 cup	vegetable oil

PREPARATION

In a pot, heat the oil over moderate heat. Fry the beef until brown. Add coconut milk. Bring to a boil. Cover with a lid and simmer over low heat for approximately 1 hour.

Take about 1/4 cup of coconut milk from the beef pot and add to a frying pan. Add the instant massamun curry paste and fry for a few seconds. Remove.

In the beef pot, add the curry paste (from step 2), fish sauce, sugar, potatoes, onion and peanuts. Simmer over low heat for another 20-30 minutes.

TIP Chicken, pork and lamb can be used instead of beef.

Phak Gad Jor
(Cabbage Soup)

PREPARATION

In a pot, bring water to a boil. Then, add the diced pork and ribs. Simmer for 15 minutes.

Then, add grounded shallots and tamarind juice. Bring to a boil. Put the pickled cabbages into the boiling soup. Simmer until cooked.

When serving, sprinkle with sauteed shallots and dried chillies.

TIP This dish is common in Northern Thailand. It is suitable for a low calorie diet.

INGREDIENTS

For 2 servings

300 g. (10 1/2 oz.)	pork, diced
500 g. (1 lb.)	spare ribs, chopped into bite-size pieces
3-4	pickled cabbages, use only the inner part
4	shallots, pounded
10	dried chillies, fried
2 tbs.	shallots, chopped and sauteed
2 tbs.	tamarind juice
3 cups	water

INGREDIENTS

For 4 servings

500g. (1 lb.)	lean pork, sliced
2 tbs.	instant red curry paste
1 cup	coconut milk, boiled
2 tbs.	crushed peanuts
1 tbs.	fish sauce
1 tbs.	sugar
2 tbs.	vegetable oil
	mint leaves, for garnishing

(Dried Red Pork Curry)

PREPARATION

In a frying pan, fry the sliced pork until slightly brown. Set aside.

Use the leftover oil in the frying pan to fry the curry paste on low heat for 2-3 minutes.

Add boiled coconut milk; stir well and add pork. Stir-fry for 2 to 3 minutes.

Add peanuts, fish sauce and sugar for taste. Cook until the pork is thoroughly done.

Garnish with mint leaves.

TIP For curry dish, meat should be fried together with curry paste and coconut milk. The meat will be much more tender. Sugar can be added if desired.

INGREDIENTS

For 2 servings

100 g. (3 1/2 oz.)	prawns, cleaned well
100 g. (3 1/2 oz.)	squid, cleaned well and cut into bite-size pieces
100 g. (3 1/2 oz.)	mussels
100 g. (3 1/2 oz.)	sea fish (sea bass, fillet), cut into bite-size pieces
100 g. (3 1/2 oz.)	crab, cut into pieces
4 cups	chicken stock
1 tbs.	lemongrass, cut into 1 cm. (1/2 inch) long pieces
2	kaffir lime leaves
5 slices	galangal
2	fresh chillies
1	dried chillies
1 tbs.	sweet basil leaves
1 tbs.	fish sauce
1 tsp.	palm sugar
3-4 tsp.	lime juice
3 tsp.	roasted chilli paste
1 tbs.	vegetable oil

Poh Taek
(Spicy Seafood Soup)

PREPARATION

In a frying pan, stir-fry the fish and seafood with roasted chilli paste for 10 seconds. Remove from heat.

In a pot, bring the chicken stock to a boil and add the seafood.

Add lemongrass, kaffir lime leaves, galangal, fresh chillies, dried chillies, and sweet basil. Bring to boil once again.

Season with fish sauce, palm sugar, and lime juice. Adjust the taste. Remove.

TIP "Poh Taek" in Thai means explosive fish wharf! Just the name itself can signify the varieties of the taste of this particular dish.

INGREDIENTS

For 2 servings

120g. (4 oz.)	chicken, sliced
3 cups	chicken stock
1/2 cup	coconut milk
1 tbs.	lime juice
1 tbs.	fish sauce
1 tbs.	lemongrass, cut into 2.5-cm.(1-inch) long pieces and pounded slightly
3	kaffir lime leaves
2 slices	galangal
2	fresh chillies, pounded slightly
	chillies, lemongrass and mushrooms for garnishing.

Tom Kha Gai
(Chicken Coconut Soup with

PREPARATION

Boil the chicken stock in a pot, and add the chicken. Boil until the chicken is thoroughly cooked.

Add coconut milk, lime juice, and fish sauce to the boiling soup.

Add the lemongrass stripes, chillies and, sliced galangal into the boiling soup.

Adjust the seasonings. There should be a pronounced sour taste, followed by a salty and hot taste.

When serving, garnish with strips of fresh chillies, lemon grass and mushrooms.

TIP Deep fried dried chillies can also be added to enrich the aroma.

INGREDIENTS

For 4 servings

350 g. (12 1/2 oz.)	beef entrails, cleaned well and cut into bite-size pieces
1 tbs.	lemongrass, pounded and cut into strips
3 slices	galangal, pounded and cut into thin slices
4	kaffir lime leaves
1 tbs.	sawtooth coriander
3-4	fresh chillies
1 tbs.	fish sauce
1 tbs.	lime juice
2 1/2 cups	water or broth

Tom Krueng Nai
(Sour Entrails Soup)

PREPARATION

In a pot, boil water or broth. Then, add beef entrails.

Add lemongrass, galangal, kaffir lime leaves, and sawtooth corianders. Stir well, and leave until the beef entrails are cooked.

Season with fish sauce, fresh chillies, and lime juice.

TIP Beef entrails can be substituted with any kind of meat.

INGREDIENTS

For 2 servings

5-7	prawns
120g. (4 oz.)	straw mushrooms
1-2	lemongrass
3-4	kaffir lime leaves
1 tbs.	roasted chilli paste
2 tbs.	fish sauce
3 tbs.	lime juice
3-4	fresh chillies
4 cups	water
	coriander leaves, red chillies and kaffir lime leaves for garnishing

(Spicy Prawn Soup)

PREPARATION

Clean and devein the prawns. Cut lengthwise down the center of the prawns, but do not cut all the way through.

Rinse the mushrooms and discard stems. Dry well, and cut in halves.

Bring the water to a boil. Add lemongrass and kaffir lime leaves; then add the prawns and mushrooms. Cook for 3-5 minutes.

Remove from heat, season with roasted chilli paste, fish sauce, lime juice, and chillies.

Garnish with red chillies, kaffir lime leaves and coriander leaves.

TIP Coconut milk can be substitued with milk to enrich creamy flavour to the soup.

Khao Yam Pak Tai

Larb Esarn

Moo Yang Nam Tok

Phla Goong

Salad Khaek

Soup Nor Mai

Tam Ma-khue Yao

Tam Tang Poo

Yam Hed Sod

Yam Hua Plee

Yam Jin Gai

Yam Moo Yor

Yam Thua Phu

Yam Woon Sen

Yam Yai

PREPARATION

In a small pot, boil all of the sauce ingredients. Simmer for 5 minutes. Remove from the heat and filter.

In a large serving platter, arrange the rest of the ingredients in separate piles.

To eat, spoon rice onto individual plates, and take a little of each ingredient to mix with the rice. Top with the sauce.

TIP Another typical southern dish for those who always wish to keep slim.

INGREDIENTS

For 2 servings

2 cups	steamed rice
2 cups	grated coconut, roasted
1/2	small pomelo, shredded
1/2 cup	dried shrimps, finely chopped
1/2 cup	beansprouts
1/2 cup	lemongrass, finely sliced
1	egg, beaten and cooked into an omelet and shredded
2	dried chilies, pounded
1 tbs.	kaffir lime leaves, finely sliced
1 tbs.	coriander, finely chopped
4-5	lime slices
Sauce:	
1 cup	water
1 tbs.	palm sugar, chopped
2	kaffir lime leaves, sliced into small pieces
2 tsp.	lemongrass, very finely sliced

INGREDIENTS

For 2 servings

200g. (7 oz.)	minced pork or minced beef
1 tbs.	uncooked sticky rice grains
2 tbs.	sawtooth coriander, finely chopped
2 tbs.	spring onion, finely chopped
2 tbs.	shallot, finely chopped
1-2 tsp.	chilli powder
1 tbs.	fish sauce
1 tbs.	lime juice
3 tbs.	boiled water
	mint leaves for garnishing

Larb Esarn
(Spicy Northeastern-style Minced Pork Salad)

PREPARATION

In a pot, bring water to a boil, add minced pork or beef. Stir over medium heat until the meat is thoroughly cooked. Remove.

In a pan with no oil, add the uncooked sticky rice grains and stir over a low heat until the rice becomes golden brown. Remove and pound roughly.

Add the pounded rice (from step 2) , chopped sawtooth coriander, shallot and spring onion to the beef or pork. Toss well and season with chilli powder, fish sauce and lime juice to taste.

Sprinkle with chopped spring onion and mint leaves for garnish.

TIP In Thailand, "larb" is usually served with steamed sticky rice and fresh vegetables such as morning glory, lettuce and long beans.

Moo Yang Nam Tok
(Spicy Marinated Pork Salad)

PREPARATION

Charcoal grill the pork until it is done. Slice into pieces.

In a mixing bowl, toss all ingredients together.

Serve with fresh vegetable as side dishes. For example, morning glory, long beans, cabbage, and mint leaves.

TIP Beef sirloin can be used instead of pork.

INGREDIENTS

For 4 servings

500 g. (1 lb.)	pork
2 tbs.	lime juice
4 tbs.	fish sauce
4 tbs.	spring onion, finely chopped
4 tbs.	shallot, finely chopped
1 tsp.	chilli powder
2 tsp.	sticky rice grains, browned
1/2 cup	mint leaves

INGREDIENTS

For 2 servings

200g. (7 oz.)	prawns
2 tbs.	lemongrass, finely chopped
3-5	fresh chillies, finely chopped
2 tbs.	shallot, finely chopped
2 tbs.	kaffir lime leaves, finely chopped
1 tbs.	lime juice
3 tsp.	fish sauce
	mint leaves for garnishing

Phla Goong
(Spicy Prawn Salad with Lemongrass)

PREPARATION

Clean the prawns and remove the back vein. Slit the prawn lengthwise without cutting in half. Boil until just cooked and set aside.

Mix lemongrass, lime juice, chillies, fish sauce, shallot, kaffir lime leaves and mint leaves together in a small bowl. This creates the spicy dressing.

Pour the spicy dressing over the prawns.

Garnish with mint leaves.

TIP Typically, Thai people use semi-cooked prawns for this particular dish.

(Mixed Salad with Curry Peanut Sauce)

PREPARATION

Clean the vegetables and drain well.

When serving, arrange the vegetables, tofu, boiled egg and chips in a serving plate.

Dress with Curry Peanut Sauce (Nam Jim Moo Satay).

TIP This dish is suitable for a vegetarian menu.

INGREDIENTS

For 2 servings

1/2 head	lettuce, medium size
1	tomato, thinly sliced
1/2 cup	beansprouts
2 tbs.	tofu cake, sliced into small pieces (optional)
1	hard boiled egg, sliced
1/2 cup	fried potato chips

INGREDIENTS

For 2 servings

1 1/2 cups	bamboo shoots, boiled and cut into small strips
1/2 tbs.	garlic, grilled and finely chopped
1/2 tbs.	shallot, grilled and finely chopped
1 tbs.	spring onions, finely chopped
1 tbs.	uncooked sticky rice grains
1 tbs.	lime juice
2 tbs.	fish sauce
1 tsp.	chilli powder
	mint leaves for garnishing

PREPARATION

Shred the bamboo shoots with a fork. Set aside.

Dry fry the sticky rice grains using medium heat. Then, pound it and set aside.

Using a mixing bowl, mix the bamboo shoots, fish sauce, lime juice, garlic, shallot, roasted rice, chilli powder and spring onions together. Adjust the flavor as desired.

When serving, garnish with mint leaves.

TIP This typical North-eastern dish should be served with steamed sticky rice.

INGREDIENTS

For 2 servings

1 1/2 cups	eggplants, grilled
1/4 cup	shallots, grilled
2 tbs.	garlic, grilled
2 tbs.	dried chillies, brown
1/4 tsp	salt
4 tbs.	vegetable oil
1 tbs.	spring onion, cut into 2.5-cm. (1-inch) long pieces
1 tbs.	coriander leaves
2 tbs.	shallots, finely chopped
2	hard boiled eggs
1/4	mint leaves

(Spicy Eggplant Salad)

PREPARATION

Remove the dark skin of the grilled eggplants, shallots and garlic.

In a mortar, pound together the eggplants, shallots, garlic and dried chillies. Add salt and pound until all mixed well.

In a frying pan, heat the oil and saute the chopped shallots until crispy and golden. Remove and set aside. In the same oil, add the mixture from step 2 and stir-fry for 20 seconds. Add spring onion, coriander leaves and half of the mint leaves. Remove.

When serving, garnish with mint leaves and crispy shallots. Accompanied with steamed sticky rice and hard boiled eggs.

TIP The eggplants, shallots and garlic can be dry fried in a pan instead of grilled.

INGREDIENTS

For 2 servings

3	salted crabs, cleaned well and drain
1	cucumber, grated length wise
3	small tomatoes, cut into halves
3	fresh chillies
3	long beans, cut into 2-cm. (1-inch) long pieces
2 tsp.	garlic, finely chopped
2 tbs.	lime juice
2 tbs.	fish sauce
1 tbs.	palm sugar
5	morning glory, for side dish
1/4	cabbage, for side dish

(Spicy Cucumber Salad with Salted Crab)

PREPARATION

In a mortar, use a pestle to pound garlic and fresh chillies together. Gradually add cucumber, long beans, and salted crabs. Alternately pound and turn with a spoon until mixed well.

Season with lime juice, fish sauce, and palm sugar. Just before removing the mixture from the mortar, add tomatoes and toss well.

When serving, accompany with fresh morning glory and cabbage.

TIP Usually served with either steamed sticky rice or Chinese spaghetti.

INGREDIENTS

For 2 servings

50 g. (1 1/2 oz.)	fresh mushrooms, cleaned and cut into small pieces
1/4 cup	onion, diced
1 tbs.	carrot, diced
4	fresh chillies, cut into strips
2 tbs.	garlic, finely chopped
1 tbs.	lime juice
1 tbs.	fish sauce
1/2 tsp.	sugar
1 tbs.	chilli sauce
1/2	tomatoes, sliced into pieces for garnishing

(Spicy Fresh Mushrooms Salad)

PREPARATION

In a mortar, pound the garlic and fresh chillies together. Then, set aside. This is the garlic mixture.

In a mixing bowl, mix together the garlic mixture, lime juice, fish sauce, sugar and chilli sauce together. Stir until well blended. This creates a spicy juice.

In a serving dish, place the onion, carrot, tomatoes and mushrooms. Then, top with the spicy juice.

TIP This dish is suitable for a low calorie diet. It contains only 80 calories.

INGREDIENTS

For 4 servings

3 cups	raw banana buds, peel and use only the inside part
1 cup	minced pork or chicken, boiled
1/2 cup	grated coconut, roasted
2 tbs.	shallot, finely chopped
2 tbs.	garlic, finely chopped
2 tbs.	roasted chilli paste
1 1/2 tbs.	fish sauce
1 1/2 tbs.	lime juice
1 tbs.	sugar
4 tbs.	vegetable oil

Yam Hua Plee
(Spicy Banana Bud Salad)

PREPARATION

Put the grated coconut in a pan with no oil. Stir over low heat until golden. Set aside.

Soak the raw banana buds in a cup of lime juice. Then slice into small pieces.

In a frying pan, heat 2 tablespoons of oil. Add shallot and saute until golden. Remove and set aside.

In a frying pan, heat another 2 tablespoons of oil. Add garlic and saute in the hot oil until golden. Remove and set aside.

In a large mixing bowl, mix the roasted chilli paste, sugar and lime juice together. Add the boiled pork or chicken, banana bud and fish sauce. Stir well.

Add roasted coconut, sauted garlic and sauted shallot. Stir well.

When serving, garnish with mint leaves and red chillies.

TIP Prawn crackers or crispy fish crackers are recommended to be served with this dish. They are available in various oriental food shops.

INGREDIENTS

For 2 servings

150 g. (5 1/2 oz.)	chicken breast, boiled and shredded
1 tsp.	garlic, finely chopped and pounded
2 tbs.	shallot, finely chopped
1 tbs.	lemongrass, sliced into 2-cm. (1-inch) long pieces
2 tbs.	spring onion, finely chopped
2 tbs.	coriander leaves
1 tsp.	chilli powder
1 1/2 tbs.	fish sauce
2 tbs.	lime juice
1 tbs.	palm sugar

Yam Jin Gai
(Spicy Northern-style Chicken Salad)

PREPARATION

In a mixing bowl, mix the garlic, fish sauce, lime juice, chilli powder and palm sugar together. This creates the spicy dressing.

Add all the ingredients to the spicy dressing. Toss until all mixed well.

When serving, garnish with coriander leaves.

TIP This is a common northern dish. "Jin" in Northern Thai dialect means small pieces. Jin Gai is small pieces of chicken.

INGREDIENTS

For 2 servings

200 g. (7 oz.)	northern-style pork sausages
1/4 cup	onion, thinly sliced
2 tbs.	lime juice
2 tsp.	garlic, finely chopped
5	fresh chillies
2 tsp.	fish sauce
1 tbs.	chilli sauce
1 tsp.	tomato, thinly sliced
	mint leaves, for garnishing

(Spicy Northern-style Pork Sausage Salad)

PREPARATION

Boil the sausage until cooked. Then, slice into thin pieces.

In a mortar, pound the garlic and fresh chillies together.

Using a mixing bowl, mix together the garlic, fresh chillies, chilli sauce, lime juice, fish sauce, and sugar. This creates the spicy dressing.

In a serving dish, top the sausages and bed of tomatoes and onions with the spicy dressing.

When serving, garnish with mint leaves and fresh chillies.

TIP Any pork or chicken sausages can also be used for this dish.

INGREDIENTS

For 2 servings

100g. (3 1/2 oz.)	pork, sliced
150g (5 1/2 oz.)	winged beans
2 tbs.	roasted peanuts, slightly pounded
1/4 cup	coconut milk
2 tbs.	fish sauce
2 tbs.	lime juice
1	dried chilli, grilled
2	shallots, grilled
1	garlic, grilled
	boiled prawns and roasted grated coconut for garnishing

PREPARATION

Using a pot, put the winged beans into the vigorously boiling water for 3 minutes. Then, remove and soak the boiled winged beans in cold water. Slice into strips.

Boil the coconut milk and remove from the pot.

In a mortar, pound the dried chilli, shallot, and garlic until blended well. This becomes the chilli mixture.

Mix the fish sauce and lime juice with the chilli mixture. This becomes the spicy juice.

Add winged beans, sliced pork, and coconut milk to the spicy juice. Adjust the seasonings as desired.

Sprinkle in the peanuts and grated coconut. Stir well.

When serving, garnish with prawns and grated coconut.

TIP Hard boiled eggs can be added to this dish.

INGREDIENTS

For 2 servings

50g. (1 1/2 oz.)	minced pork
80g. (2 1/2 oz.)	vermicelli
2 tbs.	shallot, finely chopped
1/2	onion, finely chopped
1/2 stalks	spring onion, finely chopped
2 tbs.	roasted peanuts
2-3	fresh chillies, finely chopped
2 tbs.	fish sauce
3 tbs.	lime juice
1 tbs.	sugar
	Chinese celery leaves, for garnishing

Yam Woon Sen
(Spicy Vermicelli Salad)

PREPARATION

Soak the vermicelli in water until softened. Then, boil in water until cooked. Remove from water.

Boil the minced pork until cooked. Then remove.

In a mixing bowl, mix the pork and vermicelli with shallot, onion, spring onion, chillies, fish sauce, lime juice and sugar. Adjust the flavor as desired. It should have a salty, spicy, and sour taste.

When serving, sprinkle with peanuts and garnish with Chinese celery.

TIP " Woon Sen " or vermicelli can also be substituted by instant noodle for a different flavor.

Yam Yai
(Spicy Mixed Salad)

1/2 cup	white greens, cut into bite-size pieces
1/2 cup	mint leaves
5	fresh chillies, cut into long strips
2 tsp.	garlic, finely chopped
2	coriander roots, chopped
2 tbs.	fish sauce
1 1/2 tbs.	sugar
1/4 tbs	salt
3 tbs.	lime juice

INGREDIENTS

For 4 servings

1/2 cup	pork, thinly sliced into pieces, boiled
1/2 cup	prawn, clean, remove back vein, slit lengthwise, boil
1/2 cup	pork liver, cut into small pieces, boiled
1/2 cup	pork skin, cut into small pieces, boiled
1/4 cup	chicken breast, boiled and shredded
5	quail eggs, boiled
1/2 cup	vermicelli, cut into 4-cm. (1 1/2-inch) long pieces, soaked in water until soft, boiled.
1/2 cup	dried mushroom, soaked in water and cut into pieces
2 tbs.	pickled garlic, cut into small pieces
1/2 cup	carrot, cut into small matchsticks
1/2 cup	cucumber, cut into small matchsticks

PREPARATION

In a mortar, pound the fresh chillies, garlic and coriander roots. Set aside.

In a large mixing bowl, mix together fish sauce, sugar, salt, lime juice with the mixture from step 1. Mix thoroughly. Adjust the flavour. This creates the spicy dressing.

Add pork, liver, pork skin, prawn and chicken. Toss gently. Add vermicelli, mushroom, carrot, cucumber, white greens, and mint leaves. Toss gently until mixed well.

When serving, garnish with mint leaves, fresh chillies, pickled garlic and quail eggs.

TIP Vermicelli should be soaked in water until soft before boiling. This reduces the boiling time and helps prevent overcooking.

Ab-pla

Aor Suan

Gai Phad Med Ma-muang

Goong Gra-thiam

Goong Phad Khao Pod Orn

Goong Phad Sator

Hor Mok

Hoy Lai Phad Phrik Phao

Khai Look-khoey

Khai Yad Sai

Nam Phrik Ong

Phad Fak Thong

Phad Gui-chai Pla Muek

Phad Phak Boong

Phad Phak Ruam Mit

Phad Thua Ngok

Pla Preow Wan

Pla Rad Phrik

Poo Ob Woon Sen

Poo Phad Phong Ga-ree

Pra Ram Long Song

Sa-tu Lin Wua

INGREDIENTS

For 4 servings

700 g. (1 1/2 lbs.)	fillet of freshwater fish, cut into small pieces
3 tbs.	instant red curry paste
1 cup	coconut milk
1	egg
1 tsp.	salt
2	red fresh chillies, cut into long strips
1/2 tbs.	minced galingale
1/2 tbs.	kaffir lime leaves, finely sliced
3 tbs.	sweet basil leaves
2 tbs.	coriander leaves
5	25 x 15 cm. (10 x 6 inches) banana leaves
10	toothpicks

Ab-pla
(Steamed Spicy Fish in Banana Leave)

PREPARATION

In a food processor, blend the fish with curry paste until mixed well. Remove. This becomes the fish paste.

In a mixing bowl, mix the fish paste with coconut milk, egg, salt and minced galingale. Stir until all blended well. Separate the fish paste into 5 portions.

On each banana leaf, place 1/5 of the sweet basil leaves, and top with one portion of the fish paste. Sprinkle with 1/5th of the kaffir lime leaves and fresh chillies.

Fold the banana leaf to wrap all the mixture into a rectangular shape. Secure the edges with toothpicks.

Repeat until all the fish paste is finished.

Steam the fish in the leaves in a steamer for approximately 20 minutes. Remove and char-coal-broil until the banana leaves become dark.

Serve when hot.

TIP   "Ab" in Northern Thai dialect means steamed and then charcoal-broiled.

INGREDIENTS

For 2 servings

1 cup	fresh oysters
4 tbs.	tapioca flour
2/3-1 cup	water
1	egg
1 tbs.	spring onion, finely chopped
3/4 cup	beansprouts
1/4 tsp.	ground peppercorns
2 tbs.	chilli sauce
3/4 cup	vegetable oil

Aor Suan
(Fried Oysters with Eggs)

PREPARATION

In a frying pan, heat 2 tablespoons of vegetable oil. Fry the beansprouts until cooked.

In a mixing bowl, mix the flour with water. Stir until thoroughly blended. Put the oysters in this batter.

In the frying pan, heat the remaining oil. Place the oysters and the batter in the hot oil. Stir-fry until the oysters become just cooked.

Add eggs and spring onions. Stir-fry for another 5-10 seconds or until the eggs are cooked. Remove from the heat.

When serving, sprinkle with beansprouts and peppercorns. Serve with chilli sauce.

TIP This dish should be served when very hot or on a sizzling plate.

INGREDIENTS

For 2 servings

200g. (7 oz.)	chicken breast, diced
2 tsp.	garlic , finely chopped
2 tbs.	bell pepper, cut into bite-size pieces
2 tbs.	onion, cut into bite-size pieces
2tbs.	pineapple, cut into bite-size pieces
100g. (3 1/2 oz.)	cashew nuts
3	dried chillies, cut into bite-size pieces
3 tbs.	chilli sauce
1/2 cup	tomato ketchup
1 tsp.	white soya sauce
1/4 tsp.	salt
1 tbs.	sugar
2 tbs.	vegetable oil
1 tbs.	sesame oil

Gai Phad Med Ma-muang
(Fried Chicken with Cashew Nuts)

PREPARATION

Heat the oil in a frying pan. Fry dried chillies with cashew nuts until golden brown. Remove from pan.

In the frying pan, mix the vegetable oil and sesame oil over a moderate heat. Add garlic and stir-fry.

Add chicken slices to the stir-fry.

Put onion, bell pepper and pineapple into the pan. Continue stir-frying until the chicken is cooked.

Add chilli, tomato, and white soya sauce with salt and sugar to enhance the taste. Finally, add dried chillies and cashew nuts to the stir-fry.

TIP This dish also appears on some Chinese food menus.

INGREDIENTS

For 2 servings

300g. (10 1/2 oz.)	prawns
3-4	coriander roots
2 tbs.	garlic, finely chopped
1 tbs.	peppercorns
1/3 cup	vegetable oil
2 tbs.	white soya sauce
2 tbs.	fish sauce
	coriander leaves , for garnishing.

(Fried Prawns with Garlic)

PREPARATION

Wash the prawns and then drain. Cut the center of each prawn from head to tail.

Using a mortar, pound the coriander roots, chopped garlic and peppercorns together. Mix thoroughly. Reserve some garlic for garnishing.

Marinate the prawns with the mixture from Step 2, white soya sauce and fish sauce for 30 minutes.

Put vegetable oil into a frying pan. Using medium heat, fry the prawns until they turn red. Remove the fried prawns from the pan.

For garnishing, sprinkle with some coriander leaves and crispy garlic. Crispy garlic can be made by frying the chopped garlic in vegetable oil using low heat. Fry until golden.

TIP Prawn can be substituted with fish, squid, pork or chicken.

Goong Phad Khao Pod Orn
(Fried Prawns with Baby-corn)

INGREDIENTS

For 2 servings

5-7	small prawns
50g. (1 1/2 oz.)	baby-corn, cut into 2.5-cm. (1-inch) pieces
50g. (1 1/2 oz.)	beansprouts
50g. (1 1/2 oz.)	water chestnuts (optional), cut into small dices
1	medium size onion, cut into pieces
1	green bell pepper, cut into pieces
50g. (1 1/2 oz.)	carrots, cut into 2.5 cm. (1-inch) pieces
1 tbs.	garlic, finely chopped
4 tbs.	chilli sauce
6 tbs.	tomato ketchup
3 tbs.	white soya sauce
1 tsp.	ground peppercorns
1 tbs.	sugar
5 tbs.	vegetable oil
2 tbs.	multi-purpose flour
1/2 cup	water

PREPARATION

Rinse the prawns and remove the back vein. Slit the prawns lengthwise without cutting them in half.

Dissolve the flour in water. Dip the prawns in the batter. In a frying pan, fry the dipped prawns with 3 tablespoons of oil until golden. Set the prawns aside.

Use the same frying pan to fry the garlic until golden. Add all the vegetables and stir-fry on high heat until cooked.

Season with chilli sauce, tomato ketchup, peppercorns, white soya sauce and sugar. Remove from heat.

Pour the sauce over the deep-fried prawns.

TIP Baby-corn can be substitued by snow peas.

INGREDIENTS

For 2 servings

5	small prawns, cleaned well
2 tbs.	twisted cluster beans
1 tbs.	red curry paste
2 tbs.	carrots, cut into small pieces
2	fresh chilies, sliced into strips
1 tsp.	palm sugar
1 tsp.	fish sauce
1 tsp.	white soya sauce
1 tbs.	oyster sauce
1 tbs.	vegetable oil

Goong Phad Sator

(Fried Prawns with Twisted Cluster Beans)

PREPARATION

Cut the back of the prawns lengthwise, but do not cut in half.

In a pan, use low heat to stir-fry the curry paste with the prawns. Then, season with palm sugar, fish sauce and oyster sauce.

Add twisted cluster beans. Quickly stir-fry for 5 seconds. Then, remove.

TIP "Sator" or twisted, cluster beans usually give an extremely strong smell. Squid can be included in this dish.

INGREDIENTS

For 4 servings

1	small young coconut, cut the top off to open
200 g. (7 oz.)	fillet fish, cut into small pieces
2 tbs.	white greens, boiled and cut into bite-size pieces
2 tsp.	red curry paste
1 tbs.	kaffir lime leaves, finely chopped
1 tbs.	sweet basil leaves
2 tbs.	coconut milk
1 tbs.	fish sauce
1	red fresh chilli, cut into long strips for garnishing
1 tsp.	coconut milk boiled with 1/2 tsp. rice flour, for garnishing

Hor Mok
(Steamed Mixed Seafood Cake)

PREPARATION

In the coconut, place white greens and sweet basil leaves at the bottom.

Using a food processor, mix the fish, red curry paste, kaffir lime leaves, sweet basil leaves, coconut milk, and fish sauce until thoroughly blended. Gradually add coconut milk to the mixture. This becomes the fish filling. Let it stand for 10-15 minutes.

Fill the coconut with the fish filling. Steam for 15-20 minutes.

Top with red fresh chilli and boiled coconut milk. Return to steamer for another minute, then serve.

TIP Artichokes can also be used instead of coconut.

INGREDIENTS

For 2 servings

500 g. (1 lb.)	fresh clams, cleaned well
2 tbs.	roasted chilli paste
3-4	fresh chillies, cut into long strips
2 tsp.	garlic, finely chopped
1 tbs.	fish sauce
1 tsp.	sugar
3 tbs.	vegetable oil
1/2 cup	sweet basil leaves

Hoy Lai Phad Phrik Phao

(Fried Clams in Roasted Chilli Paste)

PREPARATION

In a frying pan, heat the oil. Saute garlic in the hot oil until it becomes golden.

Add clams and stir until they are cooked.

Season with fish sauce, sugar, and roasted chilli paste.

Before removing from heat, sprinkle with sweet basil leaves and red fresh chilli. Stir-fry for another 5 seconds. Remove.

TIP The clams will open when they are cooked.

INGREDIENTS

For 2 servings

3	hard boiled eggs, peeled
3 tbs.	finely chopped small shallots
3 tbs.	palm sugar
1 tbs.	fish sauce
3 tbs.	tamarind juice
3 tbs.	vegetable oil
4	dried chillies, fried, for garnishing

(Fried Eggs with Tamarind Sauce)

PREPARATION

In a pan, fry the eggs until golden. Cut into halves and set aside.

Using the same oil, stir-fry the shallot until golden. Set aside to cool so the shallot becomes crispy.

Leaving approximately 1 tablespoon of oil in the frying pan, put palm sugar into the oil and stir-fry until it becomes sticky. Add tamarind juice and fish sauce for taste. Remove from pan.

Place the eggs on a serving plate and top with the sauce. Garnish with crispy shallots and fried dried chillies.

TIP This dish is also known as "Son-in-law Eggs" because "Look-khoey" means son-in-law.

INGREDIENTS

For 2 servings

200g. (7 oz.)	minced pork
3	eggs
2 tsp.	oyster sauce
1/3 cup	snow peas
1/3 cup	carrot, diced
3 tsp.	garlic, finely chopped
1/2 tsp.	ground peppercorns
1 tsp.	sugar
3 tbs.	vegetable oil
1 tsp.	white soya sauce
1 tsp.	fish sauce
1 tsp.	tomato ketchup
	coriander leaves and red fresh chillies for garnishing

PREPARATION

To make the stuffing, marinate the minced pork with peppercorns and white soya sauce for 20 minutes.

In a frying pan, heat the oil. Saute the garlic in the hot oil until it becomes golden.

Add the minced pork and carrots. Stir-fry until just cooked. Add the snow peas.

Season with sugar, fish sauce, and tomato ketchup. Remove and set aside.

To make the egg wrapper, heat 1 tablespoon of oil in a frying pan. Tilt the pan so that the oil covers the whole surface of the pan.

Whisk the eggs with oyster sauce. Pour the eggs to thinly cover the whole inner surface of the hot pan. Let the eggs cook until they form as a "crepe."

Place the minced pork mixture on the center of the egg crepe. Use a spatula to fold the sides of the egg crepe to wrap the filling.

When serving, garnish with coriander leaves and strips of red fresh chillies.

TIP Minced chicken can be used instead of minced pork.

INGREDIENTS

For 4 servings

200 g. (7 oz.)	minced pork
3-4	tomatoes, medium
7	dried chillies
2 tbs.	shallots
2 tbs.	garlic
2	coriander roots
2 tsp.	shrimp paste
1/4 tsp.	salt

Nam Phrik Ong
(Sauteed Minced Pork with Chillies)

PREPARATION

In a small pot, boil the tomatoes until soft. Remove from heat and peel off the skin. Quickly stir the boiled tomatoes, and set aside.

Grill the dried chillies, shallots and garlic until you can smell the aroma (Leave some garlic for frying as well.)

In a mortar, pound the grilled chillies, garlic and shallots together with the coriander roots, shrimp paste, and salt. Add minced pork and the tomatoes. Mix them together well.

In a frying pan, saute the remaining garlic, and fry the well grounded mixture (from step 3) until the pork is cooked thoroughly. If the mixture becomes too dry, add a little water. It should be a little juicy.

Just before removing from the heat, adjust the taste with fish sauce.

Serve with long beans, crispy pork skin, and fresh vegetables. For example, cabbage, cucumber, and mint leaves.

TIP This is a Northern specialty. Originally, it is usually served with steamed sticky rice.

INGREDIENTS

For 2 servings

30g. (1 oz.)	chicken breast, diced
30g. (1 oz.)	pumpkin, diced
2	fresh chillies
1 tbs.	garlic, finely chopped
1 tbs.	red basil leaves
2 tsp.	fish sauce
1/2 tsp.	sugar
1 tsp.	vegetable oil

Phad Fak Thong
(Fried Pumpkin with Chicken)

PREPARATION

Using a mortar, pound the garlic and chillies together.

In a pan, heat vegetable oil over low heat. Fry the garlic and chillies mixture in hot oil until you can smell the aroma.

Increase the heat and add chicken and pumpkin to the pan. Fry all ingredients well and season with fish sauce and sugar.

Add red basil leaves to the pan. Stir well and remove.

Garnish with fresh chillies.

TIP This dish is suitable for a low calorie diet. It contains approximately 150 calories.

INGREDIENTS

For 2 servings

100 g. (3 1/2 oz.)	Chinese chives, cut into 2.5-cm.(1-inch) pieces
50 g. (1 1/2 oz.)	squid, cleaned well
2 tsp.	garlic, finely chopped
1/2 tsp.	oyster sauce
2 tsp.	fish sauce
1/2 tsp.	sugar
1 tsp.	vegetable oil
1/2 cup	water

Phad Gui-chai Pla Muek
(Fried Squid with Chinese Chives)

PREPARATION

Clean the squid, and take out all the insides. Make thin, small cuts on the squid for decoration.

In a frying pan, use low heat to stir-fry the garlic until brown. Add the squid, and increase to medium heat. Fry the squid until it is cooked.

Add oyster sauce, fish sauce, sugar and water. Stir fry until the water starts to boil. Add the Chinese chives. Stir-fry for another minute. Remove from heat.

TIP This dish contains only 125 calories

INGREDIENTS

For 2 servings

120 g. (4 oz.)	morning glory, cleaned
1 tsp.	fermented whole soybean sauce
2 small	red fresh chillies, finely chopped
1 clove	garlic, finely chopped
2 tbs.	vegetable oil
1 tbs.	oyster sauce
1 tbs.	fish sauce
4 tbs.	water or stock
1/2 tsp.	sugar

(Sauteed Morning Glory with Fermented Whole Soybeans)

PREPARATION

In a frying pan, heat the oil over high heat. Saute the garlic until golden.

Add fresh chillies and fry. Then, quickly add the morning glory and stir-fry for 3-4 seconds.

Then, add fermented soybean sauce, oyster sauce, fish sauce, sugar and water or stock. Quick stir-fry together. Then remove from heat to maintain the fresh appearance of the morning glory.

TIP Use only red fresh chillies to contrast with the fried morning glory.

(Sauteed Mixed Vegetables)

PREPARATION

Cut the vegetables into bite-size pieces. Mix them in a bowl and put them into boiling water for a few minutes to blanch. Drain and set aside.

Heat the oil in a frying pan, and saute the garlic. Then, add the vegetables and stir-fry for approximately 2-3 minutes using high heat. Quickly fry to ensure the right texture of the vegetable.

INGREDIENTS

1/2 cup	cauliflower
1/2 cup	baby-corn
1/2 cup	snow peas
1/2 cup	carrot
1/2 cup	straw mushroom
1/2 cup	broccoli
1 tbs.	garlic, finely chopped
2 tbs.	vegetable oil
2 tbs.	oyster sauce
1/2 tsp.	ground peppercorns
1 tsp.	sugar
1 tsp.	white soya sauce

Add oyster sauce, white soya sauce and sugar to add flavor. Sprinkle with peppercorn. Fry for 1 minute.

TIP Hard-textured vegetables like cauliflower, carrot and broccoli should be pre-boiled to minimise the frying time.

(Sauteed Beansprouts)

PREPARATION
Wash and drain the beansprouts and tofu.

Heat the oil in a frying pan, and saute the garlic over high heat until golden.

Put the tofu in a pan and stir-fry. Add white soya sauce, sugar and oyster sauce to taste.

Add the beansprouts and stir-fry. Quickly remove from heat; otherwise, the beansprouts will not look white and fresh.

TIP This dish is suitable for a low calorie diet. It contains only 156 calories.

INGREDIENTS

For 2 servings

1 cup	beansprouts
1/4 cup	tofu, sliced into small pieces
1 tbs.	garlic, finely chopped
1 tbs.	white soya sauce
1/2 tsp.	sugar
1 tbs.	oyster sauce
1 tbs.	vegetable oil

INGREDIENTS

For 2-4 servings

1	whole sea fish (eg. snapper, sea-bass), cleaned well
3 tsp.	lemongrass, thinly sliced
2 tbs.	garlic, finely chopped
5-6	coriander roots
1 tsp.	whole black peppercorns
1/2 tsp.	salt
	aluminium foil, to wrap the fish
4	red fresh chillies for garnishing

(Charcoal-broiled Fish with Spicy Seafood Sauce)

PREPARATION

Remove the insides of the fish. Clean well.

In a mortar, pound lemongrass, garlic, coriander roots, peppercorns and salt together.

Stuff 2/3 of the pounded mixture (from step2) inside the fish. Rub the fish with the other 1/3 of the pounded mixture.

Wrap the whole fish with the aluminium foil. Place the fish on a barbecue and broil for approximately 15 minutes.

Serve with Nam Jim Thalay (Spicy Seafood Sauce).

TIP A large banana leaf can be used for wraping the fish instead of an aluminium foil. It should enrich the genuine "Thai Charcoal-broiled Dish" aroma.

INGREDIENTS

For 2 servings

250 g. (8 oz.)	fish, cut into pieces
2 tbs.	multi-purpose flour
1/2 cup	onion, cut into bite-size dices
1/2 cup	pineapple, cut into bite-size dices
1/2 cup	bell pepper, cut into bite-size dices
1/2 cup	cucumber, cut into bite-size dices
1/2 cup	tomato, cut into bite-size dices
2 tbs.	vegetable oil

For sweet and sour sauce:

1/4 cup	tomato ketchup
2 tbs.	vinegar
2 tbs.	sugar
1/2 tsp.	salt

Pla Preow Wan
(Sweet and Sour Fish)

PREPARATION

To make the sweet and sour sauce, mix tomato ketchup, vinegar, sugar, and salt together. Use a small pot and place over low heat. Keep stirring until it boils, and becomes caramelized. Remove from heat.

In a bowl, dissolve the flour with water. Dip the fish in the batter, then deep-fry with moderate heat until it becomes golden brown. Remove and place on absorbent papers.

In a frying pan, use moderate heat to warm half of the vegetable oil. When the oil becomes hot, add onions, pineapples, bell peppers, cucumbers, and tomatoes. Stir fry for 20 seconds, and remove from heat.

In the frying pan, use the remaining oil to saute the sweet and sour sauce until it becomes hot. Put the deep-fried fish in the pan, and stir fry for 10 seconds. Return the vegetables to the pan, and stir fry all ingredients together for another 5-10 seconds. Then, remove from heat.

TIP Prawns can be used instead of fish.

INGREDIENTS

For 4 servings

1	whole freshwater fish
1/2 cup	dried chillies, soaked in water and de-seeded
1/4 cup	garlic, finely chopped
1/4 cup	shallot, finely chopped
1/2 tbs.	roasted chillie paste
4 cups	vegetable oil
2 tsp.	fish sauce
1 tsp.	sugar
10	kaffir lime leaves, very finely sliced

(Deep-fried Fish with Chilli Sauce)

PREPARATION

Clean the fish leaving the head if desired. Drain well. Soak in salted water for 10 minutes so that it will not stick to the pan when being fried.

Make cuts about 1 cm. (1/2 inch) deep along the back of the fish for decoration.

To make the chilli sauce : in a frying pan, mix the garlic, shallot and roasted chillie paste together. Fry with 3 tablespoons of oil until you can smell the aroma.

Flavor with fish sauce and sugar. Remove from heat.

In a big frying pan, deep fry the fish until golden-brown.

When serving, place the whole fish on a serving plate and top with the chilli sauce. Sprinkle with kaffir lime leaves for garnishing.

TIP Although freshwater fish are preferred for this dish in Thailand, any good white-fleshed sea fish can be used instead.

INGREDIENTS

For 2 servings

200g. (7 oz.)	vermicelli
1	crab
100g. (3 1/2 oz.)	bacon, thinly sliced into pieces
3	coriander roots
2 tsp.	peppercorns
1 1/2 tbs.	garlic
4 tbs.	white soya sauce
2 tbs.	oyster sauce
2 tbs.	sesame oil
1 tbs.	dark soya sauce
1 tbs.	palm sugar
2 stalks	spring onion, cut into 5-cm. (2-in.) long pieces
2 stalks	Chinese celery, cut into 5-cm. (2-in.) long pieces
1/2 cup	boiled water
	coriander leaves and red chillies for garnishing

Poo Ob Woon Sen
(Casseroled Crabs with Vermicelli)

PREPARATION

Soak the vermicelli in water until softened. Then drain.

Rinse the crab well and chop into bite-size pieces.

Using a mortar, thoroughly pound the coriander roots, garlic and peppercorns. This is the herb mixture.

In a mixing bowl, season the vermicelli with white soya sauce, oyster sauce, sesame oil, dark soya sauce and palm sugar. Then, mix the ingredients.

Marinate the crab using the herb mixture for 5-10 minutes.

In a stew pot or a clay pot, place the bacon in first. Next, place the spring onion, Chinese celery, crab and vermicelli in the pot.

Pour in warm water and cover the pot with the lid. Then, heat for approximately 15-20 minutes.

When serving, garnish with coriander leaves and red chillies.

TIP Chinese cooking liqueur can be added to this dish, if available. This will enrich the herbal aroma.

Poo Phad Phong Ga-ree
(Fried Yellow Curry Crab)

INGREDIENTS

For 2 servings

1	large fresh crab
1/2 cup	coconut milk
1 tsp.	curry powder
1/4 tsp.	salt
2 tsp.	fish sauce
	spring onion and fresh chillies for garnishing

PREPARATION

Using a steamer, steam the crab until done. Cut the crab into bite-size pieces.

In a pan over high heat, heat the coconut milk and stir until it starts to boil. Add the curry powder. Fry until you can smell the aroma.

Add salt for flavor. Finally, put the crab in the pan and stir.

Quickly adjust the seasonings with fish sauce. It should give a sweet and salty taste.

When serving, garnish with spring onion cut into pieces and strips of fresh chillies.

TIP Add chinese calery when stir-fry for more aroma.

INGREDIENTS

For 2 servings

250g. (8 oz.)	chicken breast, sliced
1 tbs.	garlic cloves, pounded
1 tsp.	curry powder
1 tsp.	butter, melted
3 cups	morning glory, cut into 2-inch pieces
1 tbs.	shallot, chopped
1 tbs.	chilli powder
2 tbs.	crushed peanuts
1 tbs.	sugar
1 tsp.	fish sauce
1/2 cup	coconut milk
1 tsp.	roasted chilli paste
2 tbs.	vegetable oil
1	fresh chilli, for garnishing

Pra Ram Long Song

(Steamed Morning Glory with Sauteed Red Curry)

PREPARATION

In a mixing bowl, marinate the chicken with garlic, curry powder and butter for 1 hour.

Using a frying pan, saute the chopped shallot until golden over medium heat. Reduce the heat, and add chilli powder, peanuts , sugar, fish sauce, and coconut milk. Stir fry for 1 minute. Remove from heat.

In a pot, bring water to a boil. Put the morning glory in for 3 minutes. Drain, and place on a serving plate.

In a pan, brown the chicken using no oil until thoroughly cooked. Remove, and place on the bed of morning glory.

Pour the curry sauce over the chicken, and top with the roasted chilli paste, and chillies.

TIP The name, "Pra Ram Long Song," is derived from the hero, "Phra Ram," in Thai classical literature "Ramayana" . The green colour represents Phra Ram.

INGREDIENTS

For 4 servings

500 g. (1 lb)	ox-tongue, cleaned well
3	garn ploo or cloves
3	cardamom leaves
1	cassia, 1-inch piece
2 tsp.	salt
3 tbs.	tomato ketchup
1 tbs.	white soya sauce
1 tsp.	ground peppercorns
1 tbs.	tapioca flour
1 tbs.	wheat flour
3	onions, peeled and cut into quarters
3	potatoes, peeled and cut into bite-size pieces
2	carrots, peeled and cut into bite-size pieces
10	snow peas
3	tomatoes
1/2 cup	oil

Sa-tu Lin Wua
(Ox-tongue Stew)

PREPARATION

Clean the ox tongue well. Boil for 5 minutes. With a knife, scrape the tongue so that it looks smooth and clean. Rub the tongue with 1 teaspoon of salt and 1/2 teaspoon of ground peppercorns.

In a frying pan, heat the oil. Fry the tongue in the hot oil until brown. Remove.

In a pot, place the fried tongue. Pour the water just to cover the tongue. Add garn ploo, cardamom leaves and cassia. Simmer over a low heat for approximately 3 hours.

Remove the simmered tongue. Slice into 1 cm. (0.5 inch) pieces. Filter the soup to remove all the spices. Return the soup back to the pot.

In the soup pot, add potatoes, onion, carrots, snow peas, ox tongue, tomatoes, tomato ketchup, 1 teaspoon of salt, 1/2 teaspoon of ground peppercorns and white soya sauce. Adjust the flavour.

Dissolve the tapioca flour and wheat flour with some water. Add the flour into the soup pot. Stir well until blended. Bring the soup to the boil again. Remove from heat.

TIP Garn ploo, cardamom leaves and cassia will give a real oriental aroma to this western-origin dish

Guay Teow Lord

Guay Teow Nam Moo

Jok Moo

Khanom Jeen Nam Ngeow

Khanom Jeen Nam Yaa

Khanom Jeen Phad

Khanom Jeen Sao Nam

Khao Ga-phrao Moo Khai Dow

Khao Khai Jeow Moo Sab

Khao Man Gai

Khao Man Som Tam

Khao Mok Gai

Khao Ob Sup-pa-rod

Khao Phad Thalay

Khao Soy

Khao Suay

Macaroni Khee Mao

Mee Ga-thi

Mee Grob Rad Nah

Mee Phad Hok-gian

Mee Sa-pam

Phad Mee Korat

Phad Thai Goong Sod

Spaghetti Pla Kem

Yen Ta Fo

INGREDIENTS

For 2 servings

200 g. (7 oz.)	minced pork
300 g. (10 1/2 oz.)	flat rice noodles, steamed until soft and cooked
100 g. (3 1/2 oz.)	tofu cake, cut into small matchsticks
1 cup	beansprouts, boiled
1 tbs.	dark soya sauce
1 tbs.	sugar
1 tbs.	fish sauce
1 tbs.	garlic, finely chopped
1/2 cup	water
2 tbs.	vegetable oil

Guay Teow Lord

(Flat Rice Noodles with Minced Pork)

PREPARATION

In a frying pan, heat the oil and saute the garlic until golden. Add the pork, tofu and dark soya sauce. Stir-fry until the pork is cooked.

Add water and season with sugar and fish sauce. Adjust the flavour.

When serving, place the rice noodles in a serving plate. Top with the fried pork mixture and boiled beansprouts.

TIP This dish derives from one of the Chinese "dim-sum" dish. Prawns can be used instead of pork.

INGREDIENTS

For 2 servings

400 g. (15 oz.)	rice noodles, boiled
150 g. (5 1/2 oz.)	pork, boiled and sliced
150 g. (5 1/2 oz.)	minced pork
6	pork balls or fish balls
1 cup	beansprouts, boiled
3 tsp.	garlic, finely chopped and sauteed
3 tsp.	coriander, cut into 1-cm (1/2-inch) pieces
3 tsp.	spring onion, finely chopped
5 cups	pork stock
3 tsp.	white soya sauce

PREPARATION

Boil the rice noodles and place in a serving dish. Toss with sauteed garlic.

In a pot, heat the pork stock. Add the minced pork and pork balls. Season with white soya sauce. Bring the soup to a boil. Remove.

Top the noodles with pork slices. Pour the soup from step 2 over the noodles.

Garnish with beansprouts, coriander and spring onion.

When serving, accompany with cruet containing dishes of chilli powder, sugar, crushed peanuts, fish sauce and Phrik Nam Som (pickled chillies in vinegar) to flavour.

TIP This dish can also be served as dry noodles simply by leaving out the soup.

Jok Moo
(Pork Congee)

PREPARATION

Boil the rice in pork stock until the rice becomes completely soft.

Marinate the pork with white soya sauce and peppercorns for 20 minutes.

Using your palms, shape the pork into small balls. Add to the rice soup.

Season with white soya sauce and peppercorns, if desired.

When serving, beat the raw egg into the serving dish, then cover with the hot rice soup. Sprinkle with ginger slices, spring onion and coriander leaves.

TIP "Jok Moo" is normally served as either breakfast or supper. Pork can also be substituted with fish or chicken.

INGREDIENTS

For 2 servings

1 cup	rice, soaked in water overnight
200 g. (7 oz.)	minced pork
2 tbs.	white soya sauce
4 cups	pork stock
1 tbs.	young ginger, thinly sliced
1 tsp.	ground peppercorns
1 tbs.	spring onion, finely chopped
1-2	eggs
	coriander leaves, for garnishing

INGREDIENTS

For 2 servings

200 g. (7 oz.)	Chinese spaghetti
300 g. (10 1/2 oz.)	spare ribs, chopped into bite-size pieces
100 g. (10 1/2 oz.)	minced pork
1/4 cup	tomatoes, small
5	dried chillies
2 tsp.	shallots
2 tsp.	garlic
1 tbs.	shrimp paste
2 slices	galangal, thinly sliced
1 tsp.	lemongrass, finely sliced
1/3 tbs.	salt
2-3 cup	water

For side dishes:

1/2 cup	pickled cabbage, shredded
1/2 cup	banana bud, thinly sliced
1/2 cup	beansprouts
1/4 cup	spring onion, chopped
1/4 cup	coriander, chopped
1/4 cup	dried chillies, brown
1/4 cup	sauteed garlic
1/4 cup	lime wedges
1/2 cup	crispy pork skin

Khanom Jeen Nam Ngeow
(Chinese Spaghetti with Spare Ribs Soup)

PREPARATION

In a mortar, pound dried chillies, shallots, garlic, shrimp paste, galangal and lemongrass together until well blended. Then, set aside as the chilli paste.

In a pot, put the spare ribs and water. Using low heat, simmer for approximately 25-30 minutes.

In a frying pan, stir-fry the chilli paste (from step 1) and minced pork until you can smell the aroma. Remove from heat.

In the spare rib pot, add the fried minced pork and tomatoes. Simmer until the soup become slightly thick. Season with salt. Remove.

When serving. Prepare all the side dishes to be served with the Chinese spaghetti and the spare ribs soup.

TIP The spare ribs should be simmered in the soup long enough for them to become tender.

INGREDIENTS

For 2 servings

For fish curry:

300 g. (10 1/2 oz.)	Chinese spaghetti
500 g. (1 lb.)	fillet of fish, boiled
2 cups	coconut milk
100 g. (3 1/2 oz.)	instant red curry paste
1 tbs.	galingale, minced
2 tbs.	fish sauce
2 tsp.	shallot, grilled and pounded
2 tsp.	garlic, grilled and pounded

For side dishes:

1/4 cup	sweet basil leaves
1/4 cup	beansprouts
1/2 cup	long beans, chopped into 2.5-cm. (1-inch) long pieces
2	hard boiled eggs, cut into quarters
2 tbs.	sauteed shallots
1/2 cup	pickled cabbage, shredded

Khanom Jeen Nam Yaa
(Chinese Spaghetti with Fish Curry Soup)

PREPARATION

In a food processor, blend shallots, garlic and galingale together. Add instant red curry paste and boiled fish. Remove when thoroughly blended. This becomes the fish paste.

Over a low heat, bring the coconut milk to a boil. Add the fish paste. Stir until the fish paste is well blended with the coconut milk. Bring to a boil again. Season with fish sauce and remove.

When serving, accompany with separate side dishes of vegetables and eggs.

To eat, place the Chinese spaghetti on individual plates and pour some fish curry soup over. Top with vegetables from the side dish and toss together well with the spaghetti.

TIP "Khanom Jeen" or Chinese spaghetti dish is usually served in various merit making parties. This is because the Thais believe that the long "Khanom Jeen" noodles bring long life.

(Fried Chinese Spaghetti)

INGREDIENTS

For 2 servings

500 g. (1 lb.)	Chinese spaghetti
4 tbs.	Chinese chives, cut into 2.5-cm.(1-inch) long pieces
1 tsp.	garlic, finely chopped
2 tbs.	dark soya sauce
2 tbs.	fermented whole soybeans sauce
2 tbs.	ground black peppercorns
1/4 cup	vegetable oil

PREPARATION

In a frying pan, saute the garlic until golden. Add the Chinese spaghetti and stir-fry for 30 seconds.

Add Chinese chives, dark soya sauce, and fermented whole soybeans sauce. Stir-fry for another 1 minute.

When serving, sprinkle with ground peppercorns. Season with chilli powder, sugar, and fish sauce, if desired.

TIP This is a typical northern dish. Boiled Japanese noodles can be used as a substitute.

Khanom Jeen Sao Nam
(Chinese Spaghetti with Coconut Sauce)

PREPARATION

In a pot, bring the coconut milk to a boil. Add fish balls and prawns. Simmer until the prawns are cooked.

Season with palm sugar and fish sauce.

When serving, accompany with separate side dishes of ginger, fresh chillies, pineapple, dried shrimps and lime.

To eat, place the Chinese spaghetti on individual plates, and pour some of the coconut sauce over. Top with some of the side dishes and toss together well with the spaghetti.

TIP "Sao Nam" was originally popular in the hot season, because of its light and cool effect.

INGREDIENTS

For 2 servings

For coconut sauce:

250 g. (8 oz.)	Chinese spaghetti
8-10	fish balls
8-10	small prawns, cleaned and slit open along back
2 cup	coconut milk
2 tsp.	fish sauce
2 tsp.	palm sugar

For side dishes:

1/2 cup	young ginger, cut into thin strips
10	fresh chillies, finely chopped
1 cup	pineapple, cut into small bite-size pieces
1/2 cup	dried shrimps, minced
1/4 cup	lime wedges

INGREDIENTS

For 2 servings

2 cups	steamed rice
200g. (7 oz.)	minced pork
3-4	fresh chillies
1/2 cup	red basil leaves
2 tsp.	garlic, finely chopped
1 tbs.	oyster sauce
1 tsp.	sugar
3 tbs.	vegetable oil
2	eggs
2 tbs.	chopped spring onion

Khao Ga-phrao Moo Khai Dow
(Fried Red Basil Pork and Fried Egg with Rice)

PREPARATION

In a frying pan, heat the oil. Saute the garlic in hot oil.

Add pork and stir-fry until the pork is thoroughly cooked.

Add water. Flavor with fish sauce, oyster sauce, and sugar. Stir well.

Put in red basil leaves and chillies. Stir well for another 5 seconds and remove from heat.

In a pan, fry the egg sunny-side. Remove.

Top the rice with the fried egg. Sprinkle with chopped spring onion for garnishing.

TIP This same "Ga-phrao" dish can be made with chicken, beef, prawns or squid.

INGREDIENTS

For 2 servings

2 cups	steamed rice
3	eggs
50g. (1 1/2 oz.)	minced pork
1 tbs.	spring onion, finely chopped
1 1/2 tbs.	fish sauce
2 tbs.	water
1 tbs.	oyster sauce
3-4 tbs.	vegetable oil
1	tomato, for garnishing

(Minced Pork Omelette with Rice)

PREPARATION

Beat the eggs in a bowl with minced pork and spring onion.

Add fish sauce, water and oyster sauce to the egg mixture.

Heat the oil in a frying pan. When hot, add the egg mixture and fry until gold and crispy.

Top the warm rice with the egg. Garnish with slices of tomato.

TIP The oil should be very hot when adding the egg mixture into the frying pan. The egg will become crispy.

INGREDIENTS

For 2 servings

2 cups	rice, washed and drained well
1/2	chicken, cleaned well
1 tbs.	vegetable oil
1 tbs.	garlic, pounded
2	coriander roots, pounded
1/2 tsp.	salt
4 cups	water
For sauce:	
2	fresh chillies, finely chopped
1 tsp.	ginger, finely chopped and pounded
1 tsp.	garlic, finely chopped
1/2 tsp.	sugar
2 tbs.	fermented whole soybeans

Khao Man Gai
(Steamed Chicken Rice)

PREPARATION

In a frying pan, heat the oil. Saute the garlic in the hot oil. Then fry the rice grains until you can smell the aroma. Set aside.

In a pot, boil the water and chicken to make chicken stock.

Steam the fried rice with 3 cups of the chicken stock in an electric rice cooker. Add the coriander roots.

Arrange the rice on serving plates with portions of the chopped chicken.

To make the sauce, mix all of the ingredients for the sauce together.

Dark soya sauce can be used instead of this particular sauce.

TIP The remaining chicken stock can also be served as an accompanying side dish. Add 2-3 pieces of bite-size gourds to the stock.

INGREDIENTS

For 2 servings

For Khao Man (Coconut Milk Steamed Rice) :

1 cup	rice, cleaned well and drain
1 1/2 cups	coconut milk
2 tbs.	sugar
1/2 tsp.	salt

For Som Tam (Spicy Green Papaya Salad) :

120 g. (4 oz.)	raw green papaya, grated
2 tsp.	garlic
1 tbs.	roasted peanuts, roughly ground
1 tbs.	dried shrimps, ground
2	fresh chillies, chopped
4-5	long beans, cut into 2.5-cm.(1-inch) long pieces
1	tomato, sliced
1 tbs.	palm sugar
2 tbs.	fish sauce
2 tbs.	lime juice
1 tbs.	cashew nuts

Khao Man Som Tam

(Spicy Green Papaya Salad with Coconut Milk Steamed Rice)

PREPARATION

To cook the rice, put rice, coconut milk, sugar and salt in an electric rice cooker.

When the rice is just cooked, quickly open the rice cooker cover and stir the rice so that the coconut milk and rice mix thoroughly. Then, keep the rice warm in the cooker until serving.

In a mortar, use a pestle to pound garlic, fresh chillies, long beans, and green papaya together. Alternate between pounding and turning with a spoon until blended.

Add peanuts, dried shrimps, tomatoes, palm sugar, fish sauce and lime juice. Pound and turn with a spoon until thoroughly blended.

When serving, sprinkle with cashew nuts accompanied by the "Khao Man" (Coconut Milk Steamed Rice)

TIP Grated carrots and finely shredded white cabbage can be used instead of green papaya.

Khao Mok Gai
(Steamed Chicken Curry Rice)

PREPARATION

In a large mixing bowl, mix the chicken with yogurt, ginger, garlic, chillies, fennel, cumin, ground peppercorns, coriander seeds, cassia, cardamom pods, and cloves. Marinate the chicken with the mixture for 1 hour. (Instant curry seasoning mix can also be used instead of these herbs)

In a frying pan, fry the potatoes with half of the vegetable oil and butter until cooked. Set aside.

In the frying pan, use the remaining oil and butter to stir-fry the shallots until golden. Remove, and keep the oil to fry the rice later on.

Put the rice into boiling water for 2-3 seconds; then remove. Fry the rice in the remaining oil for 1-2 minutes. Then, set aside.

Place inside an electric rice cooker, the chicken, fried potatoes, fried shallots, and the rice in this order. Add 2 cups of water and turn on the rice cooker. Leave on for approximately 30 minutes or until the rice has cooked.

TIP When serving, garnish with fried shallots and serve with Ar-jad (cucumber sauce)

INGREDIENTS

For 4 servings

2 1/2 cups	rice, washed and drained
500 g. (1 lb.)	chicken (drum sticks and breast)
1/2 tsp.	salt
2	potatoes, peeled and cut into bite-size pieces
1/4 cup	shallot, finely chopped
1/2 cup	vegetable oil, mixed slightly with butter
1/4 cup	yogurt
1 tbs.	ginger, finely chopped
1 tbs.	garlic, finely chopped
1 tbs.	chillies , finely chopped
1 tbs.	fennel or curry powder
1 tsp.	cumin
1/2 tsp.	ground black peppercorns
1 tsp.	coriander seeds
1/2 tsp.	cassia
5	cardamom pods
4	cloves

INGREDIENTS

For 1 serving

1	pineapple, small
1	slice of ham, cut into small pieces
2	small prawns, boiled and peeled
2 tbs.	snow peas
2 tbs.	carrot, diced
1 tbs.	vegetable oil
1 cup	steamed rice
1/4 tsp.	salt
2 tsp.	white soya sauce
1/2 tsp.	ground peppercorns
1 tbs.	dried shredded pork

(Baked Fried Rice in Pineapple)

PREPARATION

Cut the pineapple in half, and scoop the insides out and save for dessert.

In a pan, fry ham, snow peas, carrots, and prawns until cooked. Then add rice. Stir-fry until mixed well, and season with salt, white soya sauce, and peppercorns. Remove from heat.

Put the fried rice in the pineapple, and sprinkle with dried shredded pork. Then, bake at 300° F for 20 minutes.

TIP   A spoonful of chilli sauce can also be added for more spicy flavour when frying the rice.

Khao Phad Thalay
(Mixed Seafood Fried Rice)

PREPARATION

In a frying pan, heat the vegetable oil. Saute garlic in hot oil until golden.

Add crab, prawns, and squid to the pan. Fry for approximately 15-20 seconds. Add rice, onion, bell pepper, spring onion, and tomatoes. Fry for another 10-15 seconds.

Season with white soya sauce and sugar. Increase the heat to high, and fry for another 5 seconds. Remove from the heat.

When serving, sprinkle with ground peppercorns and chopped spring onions.

TIP Fried rice is normally served with fresh cucumber slices, lime slices, spring onions and Nam Pla Phrik (Chillies in fish sauce)

INGREDIENTS

For 2 serving

2 cups	steamed rice
70 g. (2 oz.)	boiled squid, cleaned well and cut into pieces
6	boiled prawns, cleaned well and de-veined
1	boiled crab, clean well and chopped into pieces
2 tsp.	garlic, finely chopped
1 tbs.	spring onion, finely chopped
1	tomato, cut into small pieces
1	bell pepper, cut into small pieces
1	onion, cut into pieces
3 tbs.	white soya sauce
1 tsp.	sugar
2	vegetable oil

INGREDIENTS

For 2 servings

500 g. (1 lb.)	egg noodles
2	chicken drumsticks
4 cups	coconut milk
2 tbs.	red curry paste
2 tsp.	curry powder
1 tsp.	salt
2 tbs.	vegetable oil

For side dishes:

1-2 tbs.	shallots, finely chopped
4 tbs.	pickled cabbage, finely chopped
2-4 slices	lime
1 tbs.	roasted chilli paste
1 tbs.	dark soya sauce

Khao Soy
(Northern-style Chicken Noodles Curry Soup)

PREPARATION

Using a deep-frying pan, deep fry approximately 100g. (3 1/2 oz) of noodles until golden brown. Then, set aside for garnishing.

In a pot, brown the chicken drumstick (without oil) until it becomes cooked. Then, add salt and coconut milk. Bring to a boil while stirring constantly. Reduce the heat, and then cover the pot and simmer for 1 hour.

Using the remaining oil, stir-fry the red curry paste until you can smell the aroma. Then, add the curry powder and stir-fry for another 20 seconds.

Pour the curry mixture into the coconut milk pot. Stir and simmer for another 30 minutes using low heat.

Boil water using a large pot, and add the remaining noodles. Remove the noodles when cooked, and place in a pot of cold water for 1 minute. Then, drain.

When serving, top the boiled noodles with curry, the chicken drumsticks, and crispy noodles. Then, prepare the side dishes which include separated piles of shallots , pickled cabbage, lime slices, roasted chilli paste, and dark soya sauce.

TIP "Khao Soy" is a typical northern dish. The name "Khao Soy" came from the original "Khao Soy" noodles of the dish. However, egg noodles are mainly used today. In the recipe, beef can be used instead of chicken.

Khao Suay
(Steamed Rice)

PREPARATION

Rinse the rice well at least 3 times until the water becomes clear.

Cook in an electric rice cooker until soft.

TIP If the rice is less than 6 months old, it can be cooked using less water, since it still contains some natural moisture.

INGREDIENTS

For 2 servings

1 cup	rice
1 1/2 cups	water

Macaroni Khee Mao
(Spicy Macaroni with Chilli and Basil)

PREPARATION

In a frying pan, heat the oil and saute the garlic until golden. Add seafood. Stir well until cooked.

Season with fish sauce, white soya sauce, sugar and oyster sauce. Adjust the flavour. Add red basil leaves and fresh chillies.

Add the boiled macaroni and stir-fry. Remove from heat.

TIP Chicken or pork can be used instead of seafood.

INGREDIENTS

For 1 servings

120 g. (4 oz.)	macaroni, boiled
1/2 cup	seafood, cleaned well
1/4 cup	red basil leaves
2-3	red fresh chillies, cut into strips
2 tsp.	garlic, finely chopped
1 tbs.	fish sauce
1 tbs.	white soya sauce
1 tsp.	sugar
2 tsp.	oyster sauce
2 tsp.	vegetable oil

INGREDIENTS

For 2 servings

250 g. (8 oz.)	rice noodles, soak in water until soft then drain well
200 g. (7 oz.)	minced pork or minced prawn
1	egg, fried as omelette and then shredded
2 cups	coconut milk
1	tofu cake, cut into small matchsticks
1	red fresh chillies, cut into strips
200 g. (7 oz.)	beansprouts, remove the roots
100 g. (3 1/2 oz.)	Chinese chives, cut into 1 inch long pieces
1/4 cup	coriander leaves
1/4 cup	lime wedges
1/4 cup	shallots, finely chopped
1-2 tsp.	chilli powder
2 tbs.	sugar
1/4 cup	fermented whole soybeans
2 tbs.	tamarind juice

Mee Ga-thi
(Fried Rice Noodles with Coconut Milk)

PREPARATION

In a frying pan, over moderate heat, saute the coconut milk with spring onion. Add minced pork or prawn.

Season with fermented whole soybeans, tamarind juice, sugar and chilli powder. Add tofu and stir-fry until all mixed well. This is the coconut milk mixture.

Reserve half of the coconut milk mixture for dressing.

In the pan, stir-fry the remaining coconut mixture with the rice noodles until mixed well.

When serving, top with the reserved coconut milk dressing and sprinkle with red fresh chilli and coriander leaves.

TIP Usually accompanied with a side dish of shredded omelette, banana buds, beansprouts, chinese chives and lime wedges in separate piles.

INGREDIENTS

For 2 servings

200 g. (7 oz.)	rice noodles, soaked in water until soft
1 cup	chicken, cut into bite-size pieces
1 cup	kale, cut into bite-size pieces
1-2 tbs.	fermented whole soybeans
2 tbs.	white soya sauce
1 tbs.	oyster sauce
1 tbs.	sesame oil
1 1/2 tsp.	sugar
2 tsp.	garlic, finely chopped
2 tbs.	tapioca flour
3 cups.	water
4 cups.	vegetable oil

Mee Grob Rad Nah
(Crispy Rice Noodles with Gravy)

PREPARATION

In a deep frying pan, heat the oil. Deep fry the rice noodles until crispy. Remove and set aside.

In a pot, heat the sesame oil and saute the garlic until golden. Add the chicken and kale. Stir-fry until done.

Add water and bring to boil. Season with sugar, white soya sauce, oyster sauce and fermented whole soybeans.

Dissolve tapioca flour in some water. Add into the pot. Stir until the mixture becomes like gravy. Remove.

When serving, place the crispy noodles on a serving plate and top with the gravy. Accompany with cruet containing dishes of chilli powder, sugar, fish sauce and Phrik Nam Som (Pickled Chillies in Vinegar) to adjust taste.

TIP Beef, pork or mixed seafood can be used instead of chicken.

INGREDIENTS

For 2 servings

150 g. (5 1/2 oz.)	rice noodles, soaked in water until soft
80g. (2 1/2 oz.)	chicken breast, cut into bite-size pieces
2 tsp.	spring onion, finely chopped
2	fresh chillies, cut into pieces
1 tsp.	garlic, finely chopped
2 cups	chicken stock
2 tsp.	vegetable oil
1 tbs.	Phrik Nam Som (pickled chillies in vinegar)
1 tbs.	fish sauce
1 tbs.	sugar
1 tsp.	chilli powder

Mee Phad Hok-gian
(Fried Rice Noodles With Chicken)

PREPARATION

Boil the rice noodles. Plunge quickly into cold water and drain.

In a frying pan, heat the oil. Saute garlic in the hot oil until golden. Remove.

Boil the chicken in the chicken stock. Remove and set aside. In a mixing bowl, add the noodles and toss with garlic, thoroughly. Separate into two portions.

In a serving plate, put one portion of noodles in each plate. Top with chicken, and sprinkle with ground peppercorns and spring onion.

When serving, accompany with cruet containing dishes of chilli powder, sugar, crushed peanuts, fish sauce and Phrik Nam Som (pickled chillies in vinegar) to adjust taste.

TIP This dish is one of the Phuket's specialties. It can be served as soup noodles simply by adding in the chicken stock to the serving dish.

INGREDIENTS

For 4 servings

1/2 cup	pork, thinly slice
250 g. (8 oz.)	rice noodles, soaked in water until soft
4 cups	kale, cut into 2.5-cm. (1-inch) long pieces
2 tsp.	garlic, chopped
1 tsp.	dark soya sauce
1 tbs.	tomato ketchup
3 tbs.	fish sauce
2 tbs.	sugar

Mee Sa-pam
(Southern-style Fried Rice Noodles)

PREPARATION

In a frying pan, saute the garlic until golden using low heat.

Add pork and increase the heat to medium. Stir fry until the pork cooks. Then, add rice noodles, dark soya sauce, and tomato ketchup. Stir until all mixed thoroughly.

Add kale, and season with fish sauce and sugar. Fry until the kale becomes dark green. Then, remove.

TIP This is a specialty of Phuket. Normally, it can be served as breakfast or lunch a la carte.

INGREDIENTS

For 2servings

200g (7 oz.)	Korat rice noodles, soaked in water until soft
1/2 cup	pork, sliced
2 tbs.	garlic, finely chopped
1tbs.	shallots, finely chopped
2 tbs.	palm sugar
1/2 cup	tamarind juice
2 tbs.	fermented whole soybeans
2 tbs.	vegetable oil
1/2 cup	kale
1 tbs.	white soya sauce
1 tsp.	fish sauce
1/4 cup	beansprouts (optional)
1/2 tsp.	chilli powder

Phad Mee Korat
(Korat-style Fried Rice Noodles)

PREPARATION

In a frying pan, heat the oil and stir-fry garlic and shallot until crispy. Add pork and stir well.

Add palm sugar, tamarind juice and chilli powder. Stir-fry together.

Put in the rice noodles and fermented whole soybeans. Stir-fry until the noodles become cooked.

Add kale and season with white soya sauce and fish sauce.

Serve with beansprouts.

TIP "Mee Korat" or Korat noodles are a special kind of noodles. Rice noodles can be used instead.

INGREDIENTS

For 2 servings

300g. (10 oz.)	rice noodles, soaked in warm water for 15 minutes until soft
3-4	prawns, medium
2	eggs
1	tofu or bean curd cake, sliced into pieces
1 tbs.	ground roasted peanuts
1 tbs.	dried shrimps
2 tsp.	garlic, finely chopped
1 cup	beansprouts
2 stalks	spring onion, cut into 2.5-cm.(1-inch)long pieces.
3 tbs.	sugar
2 tbs.	fish sauce
1 tbs.	tomato ketchup
3 tbs.	tamarind juice
1/2 cup	vegetable oil

Phad Thai Goong Sod
(Fried Rice Noodles With Prawns)

PREPARATION

Heat 3 tablespoons of oil in a frying pan. Fry the garlic and add prawns. Add noodles. Keep turning the rice noodles constantly to prevent sticking. Remove when noodles are done.

In a pan, heat another 3 tablespoons of oil and fry the tofu for 2-3 minutes. Add the rice noodles and stir.

Add sugar, fish sauce, tomato ketchup and tamarind juice to the noodles. Keep frying until the noodles turn red. Then, set aside.

Put another 2 tablespoons of oil into the pan. When the oil becomes hot, break 2 eggs into the pan and scramble. Spread the egg over the pan, then put the noodles back. Mix together.

Add half of the beansprouts and spring onions to the noodles. Mix thoroughly and sprinkle with dried shrimp and peanuts.

Adjust the seasoning as desired and remove.

When serving, garnish with the remaining beansprouts and top with the prawns.

TIP To use a minimum amount of oil for frying noodles, add small amounts from time to time to prevent the noodles from drying out.

Spaghetti Pla Kem
(Thai Anchovy Spaghetti)

PREPARATION

In a frying pan, heat the olive oil and saute the garlic. Add anchovies and stir well.

Add tomatoes and peppercorns. Stir-fry until tomatoes become soft.

Add the boiled spaghetti and stir-fry with the other ingredients.

When serving, sprinkle with parsley and fried dried chillies.

TIP To boil the spaghetti for the right texture, add a pinch of salt and one teaspoon of vegetable oil to the boiling water. Boil for approximately 7-8 minutes. Stir to separate the spaghetti.

INGREDIENTS

For 1 serving

120 g. (4 oz.)	spaghetti, boiled
1-2	tomatoes, peeled and chopped
1 tbs.	anchovies
1 tbs.	garlic, pounded roughly
1 tsp.	peppercorns
2 tbs.	olive oil
1 tbs.	parsley, finely chopped
4	dried chillies, fried

(Rice Noodles in Red Soup)

INGREDIENTS

For 2 servings

1 lb.	rice noodles
2 1/2	chicken stock
50g. (1 1/5 oz.)	dried cuttlefish, boiled
5	pork, boiled and sliced
6	fishballs or porkballs, boiled
5	slices of fried tofu (optional)
1 tbs.	morning glory, cut into 5-cm. (2-inch) pieces, boiled.
50g. (1 1/5 oz.)	jelly fish, boiled
2 tsp.	salted soybean paste
2 tsp.	fish sauce
2 tsp.	sugar
1 tsp.	chilli powder
2 tsp.	vinegar or lime juice
2 tsp.	vegetable oil

PREPARATION

Soak the rice noodles in warm water until tender. Boil for 3-5 minutes. Then, remove. Put vegetable oil over the noodles, and quickly stir so that the noodles will not stick together.

In a pot, boil the fish balls, jelly fish, morning glory, and tofu with the chicken stock. Then season with salted soybean paste and sugar.

When serving, place the noodles in a serving dish and pour the soup over it. Season with fish sauce, sugar, chilli powder, and vinegar as desired.

TIP If you prefer dried "Yen Ta Fo", just exclude the chicken stock from the dish.

Ar-jad

Nam Jim Jaew

Nam Jim Moo Satay

Nam Jim Thalay

Nam Pla Phrik

Phrik Nam Som

INGREDIENTS

For 2 -4 servings

2 tbs.	sugar
1 tbs.	vinegar
1/4 tsp.	salt
2 tbs.	hot water
1 cup	cucumber, peeled and sliced into small pieces
1 small	shallot, thinly sliced
1	red fresh chilli, sliced into small rings

Ar-jad
(Cucumber Sauce)

PREPARATION

Dissolve sugar and salt in hot water. Add vinegar and allow to cool.

Place the cucumber, shallot and red fresh chilli in a small serving bowl. Pour the vinegar mixture over these ingredients.

TIP This sauce is a side dish for Moo Satay (Grilled Pork with Curry Peanut Sauce), Gaeng Ga-ree Gai (Yellow Chicken Curry) and Khanom Pang Naa Moo (Deep-fried Minced Pork Toast).

(Northeastern-style Spicy Sauce)

PREPARATION

Mix all the ingredients together.

TIP Usually accompanied with various northeastern dishes eg. Sue Rong Hai (Marinated Grilled Beef with Northeastern-style Spicy Sauce), Gai Yang & Khao Neow (Marinated Grilled Chicken with Sticky Rice) and Jaew Hon (Northeastern-style Spicy Soup)

INGREDIENTS

5 tbs.	fish sauce
2 tsp.	palm sugar
2 tsp.	tamarind juice
2 tsp.	chilli powder
1	shallot, finely chopped
1 tsp.	spring onion, finely chopped
2 tsp.	sticky rice grains, brown

(Curry Peanut Sauce)

INGREDIENTS

For 2 servings

1 tbs.	instant red curry paste
1 tbs.	roasted chilli paste
1 tbs.	sugar
2 tbs.	crushed peanuts
2 cups	coconut milk
1 tsp.	lime juice or tamarind juice
1 tsp.	salt

PREPARATION

In a frying-pan, heat coconut milk until it boils. Set aside.

In a pan, fry the red curry paste and roasted chilli paste with 2 tablespoons of coconut milk until you can smell the aroma.

Add the remaining coconut milk and stir-fry with sugar, peanuts, tamarind juice, and salt. If desired, adjust the flavor. Remove from the stove.

TIP Sometimes it is called Satay sauce. This sauce is normally served with Moo Satay (Grilled Pork with Curry Peanut Sauce) and Salad Khaek (Mixed Salad with Curry Peanut Sauce.)

(Spicy Seafood Sauce)

PREPARATION

Mix all the ingredients together. Stir until the palm sugar is well dissolved.

TIP Usually accompanied with various seafood dishes eg. Pla Phao (Charcoal-broiled Fish) , Pla Muek Ob Nei (Butter Baked Squid) and other charcoal-broiled seafood.

INGREDIENTS

1 tbs.	garlic, finely chopped
4-6	fresh chillies, pounded and finely chopped
5 tbs.	fish sauce
2 tbs.	lime juice
1 tbs.	palm sugar

Nam Pla Phrik
(Chillies in Fish Sauce)

PREPARATION
Mix all the ingredients together.

TIP Usually served with any main dish served with steamed rice.

INGREDIENTS

5 tbs.	fish sauce
1 1/2 tbs.	lime juice
6-8	fresh chillies, cut into rings
2	garlic, chopped

Phrik Nam Som
(Pickled Chillies in Vinegar)

PREPARATION

Mix all the ingredients together.

TIP Served with various noodles dishes eg. Guay Teow Nam Moo (Rice Noodles with Pork Soup), and Mee Grob Rad Nah (Crispy Rice Noodles with Gravy)

INGREDIENTS

1/4 cup	vinegar
4-5	pickled chillies, cut into small rings
1 tbs.	warm water

Gluay Khaek

Ice Cream Ga-thi

Jar Mong-kut

Khao Neow Ma-muang

Khao Phod Klook

Look Choop

Piak Poon

Phon-la-mai Loy Kaew

Sangkhaya Fak Thong

Tang Thai Nam Ga-thi

Thua Khiew Tom

Woon Ga-thi

Gluay Khaek
(Fried Bananas)

INGREDIENTS

For 4 servings

8-10	small bananas, peeled and each cut into 3-4 pieces lengthwise
1 1/2 cups	multi-purpose flour
1/2 cup	mature coconut, finely grated
1/2 cup	water
1/2 cup	sugar
1 tsp.	salt
3 tbs.	sesame seeds
2 1/2 cups	palm oil

PREPARATION

In a mixing bowl, using your hands mix the flour and grated coconut together until mixed well. Add sugar and salt to the mixture.

Add water and sesame seeds. Mix all the mixture well. Add more water if the batter appears too dry.

Dip the bananas into the batter, and allow them to sit.

Heat oil in a deep-frying pan over medium heat. When the oil is hot, deep-fry the bananas until golden brown.

Serve the bananas while they are hot. Sprinkle with sesame seeds if desired.

TIP Taro or sweet potato can be used instead of banana. Palm oil helps reduce the excess fat when deep fried.

INGREDIENTS

For 2 servings

4 cups	coconut milk
1/2 cup	sweet corn and jackfruit (if available)
1 cup	sugar
1/4 tsp.	salt
2 tsp.	gelatin
	jasmine extract

(Coconut Milk Ice Cream)

PREPARATION

In a pot, heat the coconut milk , sugar, salt and gelatin together. Add 1-2 drops of jasmine extract. Stir until all the ingredients are dissolved well. Leave until cooled.

Chill the ice cream mixture in the refrigerator for approximately 2 hours.

Pour the mixture into an ice-cream mixer and cover with lid. Churn for 30 minutes. Gradually add sweet corn and jackfruit as desired, while churning.

Top with a little light cream and peanuts when serving.

TIP Sweet corns and jackfruit should be added while churning so that they do not sink to the bottom.

INGREDIENTS

For 15-20 pieces

For the corona:

1/2 cup	dried red water melon seeds
1/2 cup	sugar
1 cup	water with 1 drop of jasmine extract

For the crown base:

1 cup	wheat flour, sifted twice
1	egg yolks
1 tbs.	butter
2 tbs.	water

For the center of the crown:

12	egg yolks
2 cups	coconut milk
2 cups	sugar
1 cup	wheat flour
	food coloring : yellow
2	thin gold sheets

Jar Mong-kut
(Sweet Miniature Crown)

PREPARATION

To prepare the corona:
In a pot, dissolve sugar in jasmine water. Bring to a boil. Let it cool.

In a brass pan, stir-fry the dried water melon seeds over low heat. Gradually add drips of the syrup (from step 1) and stir until the pan is dry. Repeat until all the syrup is finished, leaving a sugary coating on each seed.

Keep the seeds in an air-tight container. This is for the corona of each crown.

To prepare the crown base:
Knead the flour with the egg yolk and butter until soft. Add little water when the flour becomes dry.

Spread the kneaded flour into a thin sheet. Cut the flour sheet into small circles (2-cm. or 3/4-inch diameter) .

Put each circle pastry in a small chinese tea cup or a tiny pie case. Use your fingertip, press slightly in the middle so that it becomes a tiny pie base. Repeat until the pastry is finished.

Preheat the oven and bake the pie base in an oven 300 °F until cooked.

To prepare the crown center:
Mix the flour and sugar together.

Blend the egg yolks and coconut milk until well mixed. Pour the mixture into the flour.

In a brass pan, stir the mixture over the low heat. Add yellow colour when it is almost cooked or when it becomes not sticky. Keep stirring until cooked. Let it cool.

Shape the mixture into a small cherry shape. Cut into halves. Place one half on the center on each of the baked crown base.

To finish the crown base:
Dip the water melon seed into the thick syrup. Arrange around the edge of the pie base (to make the corona of the crown).

Use a fork to make cuts across each crown. Put another small bean-shape piece of yellow flour on top of the crown. Fix a little gold piece at the top. (See picture)

TIP This is one of the royal sweets. It is one of the most challenging recipes in Thai cuisine!

INGREDIENTS

For 2 servings

1 cup	sticky rice
2	ripe mangoes, peeled and cut into pieces widthwise
1/2 cup	coconut milk
1/4 cup	sugar
1/2 tsp.	salt

PREPARATION

Soak sticky rice in water for 3 hours. Strain, and place the sticky rice on the top layer of a double steamer over a thin white cloth. Cook for 25 minutes or until done. Put the rice into a covered bowl.

In a small pot, dissolve sugar and salt in coconut milk, then boil on low heat. Stir constantly. Reserve 1 tablespoon of coconut milk for topping.

Using a mixing bowl, pour the sweet coconut milk over the steamed sticky rice and quickly stir until evenly blended. The sticky rice should become slightly creamy. Cover with a lid.

When serving, place ripe mangoes beside the sticky rice. Top the sticky rice with coconut milk.

TIP This is one of the most well-known desserts of Thailand.

PREPARATION

Mix all the ingredients together in a mixing bowl.

Sprinkle with grated coconut slices for garnishing.

INGREDIENTS

1 cup	sweet corn, boiled in salted water and sliced
3 tbs.	mature coconut, grated
3 tbs.	sugar
1 tbs.	boiled coconut milk

INGREDIENTS

For 20 pieces

150 g. (5 1/2 oz.)	mung beans, wash, and soak overnight
1 1/2 cups	coconut milk
1 cup	sugar

For the coating:

1 tbs.	gelatin
2 cups	water, with 1 drop of jasmine extract
1/2 cup	sugar
20-30	4-5 inch long pointed bamboo sticks, satây sticks or long toothpicks
1	6" X 8" foam base that holds approx. 20-30 pieces of Look Choop
1-3	small paint brushes food coloring: red, yellow, green, and purple

Look Choop
(Imitation Miniature Fruits)

PREPARATION

In a pot, boil the mung beans until soft. Then, pour them through a sieve to separate the beans from the water.

Using the pot, mash the boiled beans, and add coconut milk and sugar. Stir over low heat until thoroughly blended, and until it becomes dry. Then, set aside and let cool.

To make these into fruit shapes, take about 2-3 teaspoons of mung beans and use your hands to shape them into any form of fruit you desire. For example, mango, orange, cherry, etc. Then, using the bamboo sticks, lift the fruit pieces and place them on the foam base.

To prepare the gelatin to coat the beans, use a pot and mix the gelatin, jasmine water, and sugar. Boil over low heat. Allow about 1/3 of the water to evaporate so the jelly will become thick.

Then, to coat the beans, paint the beans with the food colouring so they represent the color of each fruit. Then, leave until the paint dries. After the fruit has dried, dip them into the jelly. Dip each fruit 3 times, and let it stand on the foam base until it dries again.

When, the fruits or Look Choops are dried, use a knife to touch up the shape of them.

TIP Small leaves can be used to decorate the Look Choops to make them look real.

INGREDIENTS

For 4 servings

1/2 cup	rice flour
1 tbs.	tapioca flour
4 tbs.	burnt coconut shell water (the black colouring)
1/4 cup	coconut milk
1 cup	water
1/2 cup	palm sugar
1/2 cup	mature coconut, finely grated
1/4 tsp.	salt

(Sweet Blackened Jelly)

PREPARATION

To make the burnt coconut shell water : charcoal-grill 2-3 mature coconut shells until burnt. Pound the burnt shells roughly. Put the pounded shell into 2-3 cups of water. Let it stand until settled. The water should become dark and black. Reserve 4 tablespoons of the black colour water for colouring.

Dissolve rice flour and tapioca flour in coconut milk, water and the burnt coconut shell water (black colouring water). Add palm sugar. Stir until all mixed well and filter.

Heat the mixture from step 2 over low heat. Using a wooden spatula to stir until it forms and becomes sticky. The right texture should be very sticky that it does not drip from the wooden spatula when lifted.

Place the sticky mixture in a square plate. Let it cool.

When serving, cut into small rectangular shape. Sprinkle with grated coconut and salt.

TIP The burnt coconut shell is a typical, natural Thai black food colouring.

(Assorted Thai Fruits in Syrup)

PREPARATION

Wash the fruits well and drain. Cut into bite size dices.

Place the diced fruits in serving dishes. Add salt to syrup and pour over the fruits.

Top with crushed ice and rose petals.

Serve immediately.

INGREDIENTS

For 2 servings

Assorted Thai fruits : tangerine, grapes, pineapple, watermelon

2 cups	syrup
1/2 tsp.	salt
2 cups	crushed ice
	Rose petals, for garnishing

INGREDIENTS

For 4 servings

1	medium pumpkin
1 cup	coconut milk
3/4 cup	palm sugar
4	eggs
3/4 cup	white sugar

(Pumpkin Custard)

PREPARATION

Cut the top of the pumpkin open. Do not cut too deep and save the top of the pumpkin. Then, scoop out the insides of the pumpkin.

Beat the eggs and mix with palm and white sugar in a mixing bowl. Stir until the sugar dissolves.

Add coconut milk and keep stirring until all ingredients are blended well.

Pour the mixture into the pumpkin leaving about half an inch to the top.

Place the pumpkin on a rack in the steamer. Include the top of the pumpkin in the steamer but do not cover the open pumpkin. Steam for approximately 30-45 minutes.

When serving, cut into quarters.

TIP Pumkin can be substituted with a whole young coconut.

(Melon in Coconut Milk)

INGREDIENTS

For 2 servings

1 cup	melon, diced or scooped into balls
2 tbs.	sweet basil seeds (optional)
1 cup	coconut milk
1 1/2 cups	water
3 tbs.	palm sugar
1/2 tsp.	salt
2-3 drops	jasmine extract
	crushed ice

PREPARATION

Soak the sweet basil seeds in a cup of water for 30 minutes or until swollen.

In a large pot, boil the coconut milk and water. Add palm sugar and salt. This creates sweetened coconut milk.

If you wish, add a few drops of jasmine extract and stir well.

Arrange the fruit in a serving dish, and pour the coconut milk over the fruit. Top with crushed ice, and serve immediately.

TIP Brown sugar can be a substitute for palm sugar.

(Sweet Boiled Mung Bean)

PREPARATION

Soak the green beans in warm water for at least 3 hours or overnight.

In a large pot, boil the water.

Add the soaked green beans and brown sugar to the boiling water. Boil the beans until the beans are properly cooked or become soft.

TIP Green beans are high in protein.

INGREDIENTS

For 4 servings

1 cup	green (mung) beans
1 cup	brown sugar
5 cups	water

INGREDIENTS

For 2 servings

For Pandan Jelly :

1 tbs.	gelatin, or non-flavored jello
1 1/2 cups	jasmine water, water with 2 drops of jasmine extract
1/2 cup	sugar
8	pandan leaves, cut into 2.5-cm. (1-inch) strips

For Coconut Cream Topping :

1 1/2 cup	coconut milk
1 tbs.	gelatin, or non-flavored jello
1/4 cup	sugar
1 tsp.	salt

Woon Ga-thi
(Pandan Jelly with Coconut Cream)

PREPARATION

To make the pandan juice, use a mortar and pound the pandan leaves. Then, in a pot, boil the pandan leaves in one cup of water until the water becomes green. Pour the pandan juice through a filter to separate the leaves. Reserve 1 tablespoon of the pandan juice for the jelly.

To make the pandan jelly, dissolve gelatin in boiling water. Stir well over low heat. Then, add sugar and boil for 10 minutes. Stir continuously. Then allow it to simmer.

Put the reserved pandan juice into the boiling gelatin and stir well until it begins to vigorously boil.

Pour the mixture into a small square plate or dessert mould and let it cool until it forms.

To make the coconut milk topping, dissolve gelatin in the coconut milk and add sugar. Keep stirring well until boiled. Add salt.

While the coconut milk jelly topping is still hot, pour the topping over the slightly formed pandan jelly so that they will stick together. Then, let it cool.

Before serving, cut the jelly using a jelly cutter into small pieces.

TIP Pandan is a natural green food colouring.

Ca-fae Yen

Cha Dam Yen

Cha Yen

Nam Farang

Nam Gra-jiab

Nam Khing

Nam Ma-toom

Nam Phueng Ma-now

Nom Yen

O-liang

Phon-la-mai Pun

Punch Phon-la-mai

Ca-fae Yen
(Iced Coffee)

PREPARATION

Dissolve coffee in hot water. Add sweetened condensed milk.

When serving, add crushed ice and top with cream or sweet condensed milk.

Add some sugar if desired.

TIP The sweetened condensed milk adds a rich and creamy sweet flavour to the coffee.

INGREDIENTS

For 2 servings

4 tsp.	instant coffee
4-6 tsp.	sweetened condensed milk
2 cups	water

Cha Dam Yen
(Thai Iced Tea)

PREPARATION

Put tea leaves into boiled water, then filter.

Add sugar and lime juice. If serving cold, the taste should be strong and sweet as the ice will reduce its impact.

TIP Thai people love ice cold drinks due to the warm climate. However, this recipe can be served hot or cold.

INGREDIENTS

For 2 servings

2 tbs.	tea leaves
4-6 tsp.	sugar
4 tsp.	lime or lemon juice (optional)
2 cups	boiled water

Cha Yen
(Thai Iced Tea with Milk)

PREPARATION

Dissolve tea in hot water. Filter the tea leaves.

Add sugar and sweetened condensed milk.

Serve with crushed ice.

INGREDIENTS

For 2 servings

4 tsp.	tea leaves
4 tsp.	sugar
3 tsp.	sweetened condensed milk
2 cups	water

(Guava Juice)

PREPARATION

In a fruit blender, crush the guava and water until finely blended. Pour this mixture into a filter to get clear guava juice.

Boil the guava juice with sugar and salt at high heat. Remove and let cool.

Serve with crushed ice.

INGREDIENTS

For 4 servings

2 cups	ripe guava, cut into small pieces
6 cups	water
1/2 cup	sugar
1 tsp.	salt

Nam Gra-jiab
(Roselle Juice)

INGREDIENTS

For 2 servings

1/2 cup	dried roselle
5 cups	warm water
1 cups	sugar

PREPARATION

Rinse the roselle well and drain.

Boil water with the dried roselle for approximately 20-30 minutes using low heat.

Add sugar while boiling.

Pour the boiled roselle juice through a filter or a white thin cloth to separate the roselle. Leave until cool.

Serve with ice.

Nam Khing
(Ginger Juice)

PREPARATION

Dissolve the ginger drink in hot water.

Add brown sugar as desired.

This drink is best served warm.

INGREDIENTS

For 2 servings

2 sachets	instant ginger drink
2 cups	hot water
4 tsp.	brown sugar

(Bale Fruit Juice)

PREPARATION

Grill the bale fruit until you can smell the aroma.

In a large pot, boil the bale fruit in water at low heat for approximately 30 minutes.

Filter the boiled bale fruit juice and add sugar. Stir well until sugar dissolves.

Serve with ice.

INGREDIENTS

For 4 serving

10 slices	dried bale fruit
10 cups	water
2 cups	sugar

Nam Phueng Ma-now
(Honey-lemon Juice)

PREPARATION

Mix honey in hot water. Add lemon juice if desired.

INGREDIENTS

For 2 servings

2 cups	hot water
8 tbs.	honey
4 tbs.	lemon juice

(Pink Milk)

PREPARATION

Boil the water. Add sweetened condensed milk and strawberry syrup. Stir well until thoroughly mixed.

Serve with crushed ice and top with sweetened condensed milk.

TIP Replace sweetened condensed milk with skim milk for a low-calorie diet.

INGREDIENTS

For 2 servings

6 tbs.	concentrated strawberry or sala flavoured syrup
2 tbs.	sweetened condensed milk
2 cups	water

O-liang
(Iced Black Coffee)

PREPARATION

Dissolve coffee in hot water. Add sugar.

Serve with crushed ice.

INGREDIENTS

For 2 servings

4 tsp.	instant coffee
6 tsp.	sugar
2 cup	water

(Assorted Fruit Squash)

PREPARATION

Put all the ingredients in a fruit blender and blend thoroughly.

Chill and serve.

TIP Other fruits like papaya, banana, strawberry, young coconut and tangerine are also recommended.

INGREDIENTS

For 4 servings

1 cup	pineapple
1 cup	apple
1 cup	water melon
1 tsp.	lemon juice
1/2 cup	syrup
2 cups	crushed ice

INGREDIENTS

For 4 servings

1 1/2 cup	pineapple juice
1 cup	orange juice
1/4 cup	lemon juice
2 tbs.	honey

(Tropical Fruits Punch)

PREPARATION

Mix the three kinds of juice and honey together. Chill.

Chill and serve.

TIP Adding some Thai whiskey to the fruit punch will make "Mai Thai", a favourite Thai cocktail.

INDEX OF RECIPES AND INGREDIENTS

Published in 1999 by
Silkworm Books
54/1 Sridonchai Road, Chiang Mai 50100, Thailand.
E-mail: silkworm@pobox.com

ISBN 974-7100-83-5

Designed and produced by Firecracker Interactive, a division of Firecracker Film Co., Ltd.
Set in 9 pt. Univers 57 Condensed
Printed in Thailand by O.S. Printing House, Bangkok.